BIBLE
PROMISE
BOOK ®

Only

G OD

Edition

© 2014 by Barbour Publishing

Text selections from *Only God* © Dwight Mason.

Compiled by MariLee Parrish.

Print ISBN 978-1-62416-989-2

eBook Editions:

Adobe Digital Edition (.epub) 978-1-63058-045-2

Kindle and MobiPocket Edition (.prc) 978-1-63058-046-9

Scripture quotations marked KJV are taken from the King James Version of the Bible.

Scripture quotations marked NIV are taken from the HOLY BIBLE, NEW INTERNATIONAL VERSION®. NIV®. Copyright © 1973, 1978, 1984, 2011 by Biblica, Inc.™ Used by permission. All rights reserved worldwide.

Scripture quotations marked MSG are from *THE MESSAGE*. Copyright © by Eugene H. Peterson 1993, 1994, 1995, 1996, 2000, 2001, 2002. Used by permission of NavPress Publishing Group.

Scripture quotations marked NLV are taken from the Holy Bible, New Life Version. Copyright © 1969, 1976, 1978, 1983, 1986, by Christian Literature International, P.O. Box 777, Canby, OR 97103. Used by permission.

Scripture quotations marked NLT are taken from the *Holy Bible*. New Living Translation copyright© 1996, 2004, 2007 by Tyndale House Foundation. Used by permission of Tyndale House Publishers, Inc. Carol Stream, Illinois 60188. All rights reserved.

Scripture quotations marked NASB are taken from the New American Standard Bible,® Copyright© 1960, 1962, 1963, 1968, 1971, 1972, 1973, 1975, 1977, 1995 by The Lockman Foundation. Used by permission.

Scripture quotations marked NCV are taken from the New Century Version of the Bible, copyright © 2005 by Thomas Nelson, Inc. Used by permission. All rights reserved.

Scripture quotations marked AMP are taken from the Amplified® Bible, © 1954, 1958, 1962, 1964, 1965, 1987 by The Lockman Foundation. Used by permission.

Scripture quotations marked ESV are from The Holy Bible, English Standard Version®, copyright © 2001 by Crossway Bibles, a publishing ministry of Good News Publishers. Used by permission. All rights reserved.

Scripture quotations marked CEV are from the Contemporary English Version, Copyright © 1995 by American Bible Society. Used by permission.

Published by Barbour Publishing, Inc., P.O. Box 719, Uhrichsville, Ohio 44683, www.barbourbooks.com

Our mission is to publish and distribute inspirational products offering exceptional value and biblical encouragement to the masses.

Member of the
Evangelical Christian
Publishers Association

Printed in the United States of America.

THE
BIBLE
PROMISE
BOOK®

Only

GOD

Edition

<small>DWIGHT MASON</small>

<small>BARBOUR</small>
PUBLISHING

CONTENTS

INTRODUCTION

God's Word is full of promises.
And you know when He makes a promise,
you can trust it—*always*!

*These inspiring Bible promises
will renew and refresh your soul!*

Each topic in this promise book was inspired by the powerful, life-transforming title *Only God: Change Your Story, Change the World* by Dwight Mason— in which readers are encouraged and challenged to let God work in and through them to change their world.

Allow each scripture selection to speak directly to your heart, as you draw ever closer to your heavenly Father.

THE PUBLISHERS

YOUR CHALLENGES

Changing our desires and embracing change is almost always inconvenient. If we aren't willing to embrace the changes, we'll never experience the miracle. What is it about your focus that needs to change? What has occupied your greatest thoughts and energy up to right now? How about your beliefs? What needs to change in those areas? Is Jesus a "good guy," someone you like to hang with when it's convenient or when you need a miracle. . .or is He *Master*? To whom are you listening? What are the other voices telling you? What would it mean for you to hear and obey the voice of Jesus above all else?

"Only God" stories start right here—in the exact moment we stop running and resisting. . .and *embrace* change.

Consider it a sheer gift, friends, when tests and challenges come at you from all sides. You know that under pressure, your faith-life is forced into the open and shows its true colors. So don't try to get out of anything prematurely. Let it do its work so you become mature and well-developed, not deficient in any way.

JAMES 1:2–4 MSG

Dear friends, do not be surprised at the fiery ordeal
that has come on you to test you, as though something
strange were happening to you. But rejoice inasmuch as
you participate in the sufferings of Christ, so that you
may be overjoyed when his glory is revealed.

1 PETER 4:12–13 NIV

Cast all your anxiety on him because he cares for you.

1 PETER 5:7 NIV

May God, who gives this patience and encouragement, help
you live in complete harmony with each other, as is fitting for
followers of Christ Jesus. Then all of you can join together
with one voice, giving praise and glory to God, the Father of
our Lord Jesus Christ. Therefore, accept each other just as
Christ has accepted you so that God will be given glory.

ROMANS 15:5–7 NLT

You have this faith and love because of your hope, and what
you hope for is kept safe for you in heaven. You learned about
this hope when you heard the message about the truth, the
Good News that was told to you. Everywhere in the world
that Good News is bringing blessings and is growing. This has
happened with you, too, since you heard the Good News and
understood the truth about the grace of God.

COLOSSIANS 1:5–6 NCV

We who are strong must be considerate of those who are sensitive about things like this. We must not just please ourselves. We should help others do what is right and build them up in the Lord. For even Christ didn't live to please himself. As the Scriptures say, "The insults of those who insult you, O God, have fallen on me." Such things were written in the Scriptures long ago to teach us. And the Scriptures give us hope and encouragement as we wait patiently for God's promises to be fulfilled.

ROMANS 15:1–4 NLT

Then Jesus told his disciples a parable to show them that they should always pray and not give up.

LUKE 18:1 NIV

Don't worry about anything; instead, pray about everything. Tell God what you need, and thank him for all he has done. Then you will experience God's peace, which exceeds anything we can understand. His peace will guard your hearts and minds as you live in Christ Jesus.

PHILIPPIANS 4:6–7 NLT

The LORD replied, "Don't say, 'I'm too young,' for you must go wherever I send you and say whatever I tell you. And don't be afraid of the people, for I will be with you and will protect you. I, the LORD, have spoken!"

JEREMIAH 1:7–8 NLT

I lift up my eyes to the mountains—where does my help come
from? My help comes from the LORD, the Maker of heaven
and earth. He will not let your foot slip—he who
watches over you will not slumber.

PSALM 121:1–3 NIV

In his grace, God has given us different gifts for doing certain
things well. So if God has given you the ability to prophesy,
speak out with as much faith as God has given you. If your
gift is serving others, serve them well. If you are a teacher,
teach well. If your gift is to encourage others, be encouraging.
If it is giving, give generously. If God has given you leadership
ability, take the responsibility seriously. And if you have a gift
for showing kindness to others, do it gladly.

ROMANS 12:6–8 NLT

"Don't be afraid," he said, "for you are very precious to God.
Peace! Be encouraged! Be strong!" As he spoke these words to
me, I suddenly felt stronger and said to him, "Please speak to
me, my lord, for you have strengthened me."

DANIEL 10:19 NLT

Whom have I in heaven but you?
And there is nothing on earth that I desire besides you.
My flesh and my heart may fail,
but God is the strength of my heart and my portion forever.

PSALM 73:25–26 ESV

Help me understand the meaning of your commandments,
and I will meditate on your wonderful deeds. I weep with
sorrow; encourage me by your word.

PSALM119:27–28 NLT

And let the peace that comes from Christ rule in your hearts.
For as members of one body you are called to
live in peace. And always be thankful.

COLOSSIANS 3:15 NLT

My help comes from the LORD, who made heaven and earth!
He will not let you stumble; the one who watches over you
will not slumber. Indeed, he who watches over Israel never
slumbers or sleeps. The LORD himself watches over you!

PSALM 121:2–5 NLT

"Ask, and it will be given to you; seek, and you will find;
knock, and it will be opened to you. For everyone who asks
receives, and the one who seeks finds, and to the
one who knocks it will be opened."

MATTHEW 7:7–8 ESV

You will always harvest what you plant. Those who live only
to satisfy their own sinful nature will harvest decay and death
from that sinful nature. But those who live to please the Spirit
will harvest everlasting life from the Spirit.

GALATIANS 6:7–8 NLT

May our Lord Jesus Christ himself and God our Father
encourage you and strengthen you in every good thing you
do and say. God loved us, and through his grace he gave us a
good hope and encouragement that continues forever.

2 Thessalonians 2:16–17 ncv

No temptation has overtaken you that is not common to man.
God is faithful, and he will not let you be tempted beyond
your ability, but with the temptation he will also provide the
way of escape, that you may be able to endure it.

1 Corinthians 10:13 esv

"The Lord your God is with you, the Mighty Warrior who
saves. He will take great delight in you; in his love he will no
longer rebuke you, but will rejoice over you with singing."

Zephaniah 3:17 niv

So we have been greatly encouraged in the midst of our
troubles and suffering, dear brothers and sisters, because you
have remained strong in your faith. It gives us new life to
know that you are standing firm in the Lord.

1 Thessalonians 3:7–8 nlt

The law of Moses was unable to save us because of the weakness of our sinful nature. So God did what the law could not do. He sent his own Son in a body like the bodies we sinners have. And in that body God declared an end to sin's control over us by giving his Son as a sacrifice for our sins.

ROMANS 8:3 NLT

You are my hiding place; you will protect me from trouble and surround me with songs of deliverance.
I will instruct you and teach you in the way you should go; I will counsel you with my loving eye on you.

PSALM 32:7–8 NIV

But I trust in you, LORD; I say, "You are my God."
My times are in your hands; deliver me from the hands of my enemies, from those who pursue me.

PSALM 31:14–15 NIV

The LORD gives his people strength.
The LORD blesses them with peace.

PSALM 29:11 NLT

You keep him in perfect peace whose mind is stayed on you, because he trusts in you. Trust in the LORD forever, for the LORD GOD is an everlasting rock.

ISAIAH 26:3–4 ESV

"Peace I leave with you; my peace I give you.
I do not give to you as the world gives. Do not let
your hearts be troubled and do not be afraid."
JOHN 14:27 NIV

So then we pursue the things which make for
peace and the building up of one another.
ROMANS 14:19 NASB

For God was pleased to have all his fullness dwell in him, and
through him to reconcile to himself all things, whether things
on earth or things in heaven, by making peace through
his blood, shed on the cross.
COLOSSIANS 1:19–20 NIV

May God himself, the God of peace, sanctify you through
and through. May your whole spirit, soul and body be kept
blameless at the coming of our Lord Jesus Christ. The one
who calls you is faithful, and he will do it.
1 THESSALONIANS 5:23–24 NIV

Now may the Lord of peace himself give you peace at all
times and in every way. The Lord be with all of you.
2 THESSALONIANS 3:16 NIV

I trust in you; do not let me be put to shame, nor let my
enemies triumph over me. No one who hopes in you
will ever be put to shame, but shame will come on those
who are treacherous without cause. Show me
your ways, Lord, teach me your paths.
PSALM 25:2–4 NIV

Many are the plans in a person's heart,
but it is the Lord's purpose that prevails.
PROVERBS 19:21 NIV

Guide me in your truth and teach me,
for you are God my Savior,
and my hope is in you all day long.
PSALM 25:5 NIV

Protect me and save me.
I trust you, so do not let me be disgraced.
My hope is in you,
so may goodness and honesty guard me.
PSALM 25:21–22 NCV

"For I know the plans I have for you," declares the Lord,
"plans to prosper you and not to harm you,
plans to give you hope and a future."
JEREMIAH 29:11

We put our hope in the LORD. He is our help and our shield.
In him our hearts rejoice, for we trust in his holy name.

PSALM 33:20–21 NLT

Let your unfailing love surround us, LORD,
for our hope is in you alone.

PSALM 33:22 NLT

Why am I so sad? Why am I so upset?
I should put my hope in God and keep praising him,
my Savior and my God.

PSALM 42:5–6 NCV

Remember your promise to me;
it is my only hope.
Your promise revives me;
it comforts me in all my troubles.

PSALM 119:49–50 NLT

I am counting on the LORD;
yes, I am counting on him.
I have put my hope in his word.

PSALM 130:5 NLT

"Then you will call on me and come and pray to me, and I
will listen to you. You will seek me and find me
when you seek me with all your heart."

JEREMIAH 29:12–13 NIV

But this I call to mind, and therefore I have hope:
The steadfast love of the LORD never ceases; his mercies
never come to an end; they are new every morning; great is
your faithfulness. "The LORD is my portion," says my soul,
"therefore I will hope in him." The LORD is good to those who
wait for him, to the soul who seeks him.

LAMENTATIONS 3:21–25 ESV

Never be lacking in zeal, but keep your spiritual fervor,
serving the Lord. Be joyful in hope, patient in
affliction, faithful in prayer.

ROMANS 12:11–12 NIV

Such things were written in the Scriptures long ago to teach
us. And the Scriptures give us hope and encouragement as we
wait patiently for God's promises to be fulfilled.

ROMANS 15:4 NLT

But we have the true hope that comes from being made right
with God, and by the Spirit we wait eagerly for this hope.

GALATIANS 5:5 NCV

Now may our Lord Jesus Christ himself, and God our Father,
who loved us and gave us eternal comfort and good hope
through grace, comfort your hearts and establish
them in every good work and word.

2 THESSALONIANS 2:16–17 ESV

YOUR CHOICES

Never underestimate the implications of an apparently small change in your plotline. Think for a moment. If you could change one event in your story up to this point, what would it be? Some of us would have asked that girl to the prom. Some of us wouldn't have asked the girl we did. Some of us wouldn't have chosen to go to that school. Some of us would. . . Well, you get the idea.

I have come to realize that there truly are no "small" moments or "small" decisions. Even what may seem like the most insignificant decisions we make affect our entire lives—for good or for bad. Each moment of your life affects the next, and the next, and so on. Each choice we make, every moment we live, is a part of a chain of events that ultimately made us who we are and directed our life story to this point.

So whether you eat or drink or whatever you do, do it all for the glory of God.
1 Corinthians 10:31 NIV

This day I call the heavens and the earth as witnesses
against you that I have set before you life and death,
blessings and curses. Now choose life, so that
you and your children may live.

DEUTERONOMY 30:19 NIV

To choose life is to love the LORD your God, obey him,
and stay close to him. He is your life, and he will let you
live many years in the land, the land he promised to give
your ancestors Abraham, Isaac, and Jacob.

DEUTERONOMY 30:20 NCV

"Now therefore fear the LORD and serve him in sincerity
and in faithfulness. Put away the gods that your fathers
served beyond the River and in Egypt, and serve the
LORD. And if it is evil in your eyes to serve the LORD,
choose this day whom you will serve, whether the gods
your fathers served in the region beyond the River, or
the gods of the Amorites in whose land you dwell. But as
for me and my house, we will serve the LORD."

JOSHUA 24:14–15 ESV

It is better to get wisdom than gold,
and to choose understanding rather than silver!
Good people stay away from evil.
By watching what they do, they protect their lives.

PROVERBS 16:16–17 NCV

For your name's sake, O LORD,
pardon my guilt, for it is great.
Who is the man who fears the LORD?
Him will he instruct in the way that he should choose.
His soul shall abide in well-being,
and his offspring shall inherit the land.
PSALM 25:11–13 ESV

I choose the true road to Somewhere,
I post your road signs at every curve and corner.
I grasp and cling to whatever you tell me;
GOD, don't let me down!
I'll run the course you lay out for me
if you'll just show me how.
PSALM 119:30–32 MSG

"Then you will call to me, but I will not answer.
You will look for me, but you will not find me. It is because
you rejected knowledge and did not choose to respect the
LORD. You did not accept my advice, and you rejected my
correction. So you will get what you deserve; you will get
what you planned for others. Fools will die because they
refuse to listen; they will be destroyed because they do not
care. But those who listen to me will live in safety
and be at peace, without fear of injury."
PROVERBS 1:28–33 NCV

Do not accuse anyone for no reason—
when they have done you no harm.
Do not envy the violent
or choose any of their ways.
For the LORD detests the perverse
but takes the upright into his confidence.
PROVERBS 3:30–32 NIV

People with good sense know what I say is true;
and those with knowledge know my words are right.
Choose my teachings instead of silver,
and knowledge rather than the finest gold.
Wisdom is more precious than rubies.
Nothing you could want is equal to it.
PROVERBS 8:9–11 NCV

"I no longer call you servants, because a servant does not
know his master's business. Instead, I have called you friends,
for everything that I learned from my Father I have made
known to you. You did not choose me, but I chose you and
appointed you so that you might go and bear fruit—fruit
that will last—and so that whatever you ask in my name the
Father will give you. This is my command: Love each other."
JOHN 15:15–17 NIV

"'I'm sending you off to open the eyes of the outsiders so they can see the difference between dark and light, and choose light, see the difference between Satan and God, and choose God. I'm sending you off to present my offer of sins forgiven, and a place in the family, inviting them into the company of those who begin real living by believing in me.'"

ACTS 26:17–18 MSG

My choice is you, GOD, first and only.
And now I find I'm *your* choice!
You set me up with a house and yard.
And then you made me your heir!

PSALM 16:5–6 MSG

My counsel is this: Live freely, animated and motivated by God's Spirit. Then you won't feed the compulsions of selfishness. For there is a root of sinful self-interest in us that is at odds with a free spirit, just as the free spirit is incompatible with selfishness. These two ways of life are antithetical, so that you cannot live at times one way and at times another way according to how you feel on any given day. Why don't you choose to be led by the Spirit and so escape the erratic compulsions of a law-dominated existence?

GALATIANS 5:16–18 MSG

This is my prayer for you: that your love will grow more
and more; that you will have knowledge and understanding
with your love; that you will see the difference between good
and bad and will choose the good; that you will be pure and
without wrong for the coming of Christ; that you will do
many good things with the help of Christ to
bring glory and praise to God.

PHILIPPIANS 1:9–11 NCV

Trust in the LORD with all your heart and lean not on your
own understanding; in all your ways submit to him,
and he will make your paths straight.

PROVERBS 3:5–6 NIV

Your word is a lamp for my feet, a light on my path.
The unfolding of your words gives light;
it gives understanding to the simple.

PSALM 119:105, 130 NIV

Therefore, I urge you, brothers and sisters, in view of
God's mercy, to offer your bodies as a living sacrifice,
holy and pleasing to God—this is your true and proper
worship. Do not conform to the pattern of this world,
but be transformed by the renewing of your mind. Then
you will be able to test and approve what God's will is—
his good, pleasing and perfect will.

ROMANS 12:1–2 NIV

The instructions of the LORD are perfect, reviving the soul.
The decrees of the LORD are trustworthy, making wise the
simple. The commandments of the LORD are right,
bringing joy to the heart. The commands of the
LORD are clear, giving insight for living.
PSALM 19:7–8 NLT

Whatever you do, work at it with all your heart, as working
for the Lord, not human masters, since you know that you
will receive an inheritance from the Lord as a reward.
It is the Lord Christ you are serving.
COLOSSIANS 3:23–24 NIV

Don't let anyone capture you with empty philosophies and
high-sounding nonsense that come from human thinking
and from the spiritual powers of this world, rather than from
Christ. For in Christ lives all the fullness of God in a human
body. So you also are complete through your union with
Christ, who is the head over every ruler and authority.
COLOSSIANS 2:8–10 NLT

They are to do good, to be rich in good works, to be generous
and ready to share, thus storing up treasure for themselves as
a good foundation for the future, so that they may take
hold of that which is truly life.
1 TIMOTHY 6:18–19 ESV

A sluggard's appetite is never filled,
but the desires of the diligent are fully satisfied.

PROVERBS 13:4 NIV

Don't befriend angry people
or associate with hot-tempered people,
or you will learn to be like them
and endanger your soul.

PROVERBS 22:24–25 NLT

If you plan to do evil, you will be lost; if you plan to do good,
you will receive unfailing love and faithfulness.
Work brings profit, but mere talk leads to poverty!
Wealth is a crown for the wise;
the effort of fools yields only foolishness.

PROVERBS 14:22–24 NLT

One of the teachers of religious law was standing there
listening to the debate. He realized that Jesus had answered
well, so he asked, "Of all the commandments, which is
the most important?" Jesus replied, "The most important
commandment is this: 'Listen, O Israel! The LORD our God is
the one and only LORD. And you must love the LORD your God
with all your heart, all your soul, all your mind, and all your
strength.' The second is equally important: 'Love your neighbor
as yourself.' No other commandment is greater than these."

MARK 12:28–31 NLT

To know wisdom and instruction,
to understand words of insight,
to receive instruction in wise dealing,
in righteousness, justice, and equity;
to give prudence to the simple,
knowledge and discretion to the youth—
Let the wise hear and increase in learning,
and the one who understands obtain guidance…
The fear of the LORD is the beginning of knowledge;
fools despise wisdom and instruction.

PROVERBS 1:2–5, 7 ESV

If you declare with your mouth, "Jesus is Lord," and believe
in your heart that God raised him from the dead, you will
be saved. For it is with your heart that you believe and are
justified, and it is with your mouth that you profess your
faith and are saved. As Scripture says, "Anyone who believes
in him will never be put to shame." For there is no difference
between Jew and Gentile—the same Lord is Lord of all and
richly blesses all who call on him, for, "Everyone who calls on
the name of the Lord will be saved."

ROMANS 10:9–13 NIV

Good planning and hard work lead to prosperity,
but hasty shortcuts lead to poverty.
Wealth created by a lying tongue
is a vanishing mist and a deadly trap.

PROVERBS 21:5–6 NLT

Walk in obedience to all that the Lord your God has commanded you, so that you may live and prosper and prolong your days in the land that you will possess.

Deuteronomy 5:33 niv

"So do not worry, saying, 'What shall we eat?' or 'What shall we drink?' or 'What shall we wear?' For the pagans run after all these things, and your heavenly Father knows that you need them. But seek first his kingdom and his righteousness, and all these things will be given to you as well."

Matthew 6:31–33 niv

But from everlasting to everlasting
the Lord's love is with those who fear him,
and his righteousness with their children's children—
with those who keep his covenant
and remember to obey his precepts.

Psalm 103:17–18 niv

But the Lord watches over those who fear him, those who rely on his unfailing love. He rescues them from death and keeps them alive in times of famine. We put our hope in the Lord. He is our help and our shield. In him our hearts rejoice, for we trust in his holy name. Let your unfailing love surround us, Lord, for our hope is in you alone.

Psalm 33:18–22 nlt

A joyful heart makes a cheerful face, But when the heart is sad, the spirit is broken. The mind of the intelligent seeks knowledge, But the mouth of fools feeds on folly. All the days of the afflicted are bad, But a cheerful heart *has* a continual feast. Better is a little with the fear of the LORD Than great treasure and turmoil with it.

PROVERBS 15:13–16 NASB

The wicked earns deceptive wages,
But he who sows righteousness *gets* a true reward.

PROVERBS 11:18 NASB

To humans belong the plans of the heart,
but from the LORD comes the proper answer of the tongue.
All a person's ways seem pure to them,
but motives are weighed by the LORD.
Commit to the LORD whatever you do,
and he will establish your plans.
The LORD works out everything to its proper end—
even the wicked for a day of disaster.
The LORD detests all the proud of heart.
Be sure of this: They will not go unpunished.
Through love and faithfulness sin is atoned for;
through the fear of the LORD evil is avoided.
When the LORD takes pleasure in anyone's way,
he causes their enemies to make peace with them.

PROVERBS 16:1–7 NIV

YOUR DREAMS

Without a doubt, the most heart-thumping, adrenaline-pumping risk I ever take is to share my yearnings, my dreams, my God-given passions with someone who has the capacity to help me, and to ask that person to join me in changing the world.

This part of the adventure keeps me totally dependent on God. I am reminded to depend on Him every time I ask someone to take a leap of faith and buy in to something unproven but so big only God can accomplish it. When I do that, I am giving someone an opportunity to first believe in my integrity and that I have done my homework, and then to believe that God has spoken to me and is now speaking to them through me. I never get past how weighty all that really is. However, I also never get past the greater facts that God has put these yearnings in my heart for a reason, and that the greatest thing I can do for myself and for others is to be obedient to Him.

"But the seed planted in the good earth represents those who hear the Word, embrace it, and produce a harvest beyond their wildest dreams."

MARK 4:20 MSG

"You'll know then that I am God.
No one who hopes in me ever regrets it."
ISAIAH 49:23 MSG

My aim is to raise hopes by pointing the way to life without
end. This is the life God promised long ago—and he doesn't
break promises! And then when the time was ripe, he went
public with his truth. I've been entrusted to proclaim this
Message by order of our Savior, God himself.
TITUS 1:2–3 MSG

As for the rich in this present age, charge them not to be
haughty, nor to set their hopes on the uncertainty of riches,
but on God, who richly provides us with everything to enjoy.
1 TIMOTHY 6:17 ESV

Love bears all things, believes all things,
hopes all things, endures all things.
1 CORINTHIANS 13:7 ESV

Now faith is being sure we will get what we hope for.
It is being sure of what we cannot see.
HEBREWS 11:1 NLV

"Bring your full tithe to the Temple treasury so there will be
ample provisions in my Temple. Test me in this and see if
I don't open up heaven itself to you and pour out blessings
beyond your wildest dreams."
MALACHI 3:9–10 MSG

" 'Risk your life and get more than you ever dreamed of.
Play it safe and end up holding the bag.' "
LUKE 19:26 MSG

God can do anything, you know—far more than you could
ever imagine or guess or request in your wildest dreams! He
does it not by pushing us around but by working within us,
his Spirit deeply and gently within us.
EPHESIANS 3:20 MSG

In the same way, wisdom is sweet to your soul.
If you find it, you will have a bright future,
and your hopes will not be cut short.
PROVERBS 24:14 NLT

GOD makes everything come out right; he puts victims back on their feet. He showed Moses how he went about his work, opened up his plans to all Israel. GOD is sheer mercy and grace; not easily angered, he's rich in love. He doesn't endlessly nag and scold, nor hold grudges forever. He doesn't treat us as our sins deserve, nor pay us back in full for our wrongs. As high as heaven is over the earth, so strong is his love to those who fear him. And as far as sunrise is from sunset, he has separated us from our sins. As parents feel for their children, GOD feels for those who fear him. He knows us inside and out, keeps in mind that we're made of mud. Men and women don't live very long; like wildflowers they spring up and blossom, But a storm snuffs them out just as quickly, leaving nothing to show they were here. GOD's love, though, is ever and always, eternally present to all who fear him, Making everything right for them and their children as they follow his Covenant ways and remember to do whatever he said.

PSALM 103:6–18 MSG

Happy is the person who trusts the LORD, who doesn't turn
to those who are proud or to those who worship false gods.
LORD my God, you have done many miracles.
Your plans for us are many. If I tried to tell them all,
there would be too many to count.
PSALM 40:4–5 NCV

And we believers also groan, even though we have the Holy
Spirit within us as a foretaste of future glory, for we long for
our bodies to be released from sin and suffering. We, too,
wait with eager hope for the day when God will give us our
full rights as his adopted children, including the new bodies
he has promised us. We were given this hope when we were
saved. (If we already have something, we don't need to hope
for it. But if we look forward to something we don't yet have,
we must wait patiently and confidently.)
ROMANS 8:23–25 NLT

But we have the true hope that comes from being made right
with God, and by the Spirit we wait eagerly for this hope.
GALATIANS 5:5 NCV

The plans of hard-working people earn a profit.
PROVERBS 21:5 NCV

Guide me in your truth and teach me,
for you are God my Savior,
and my hope is in you all day long.
PSALM 25:5 NIV

Plans fail without good advice,
but they succeed with the advice of many others.
PROVERBS 15:22 NCV

People may make plans in their minds,
but only the LORD can make them come true.
You may believe you are doing right,
but the LORD will judge your reasons.
Depend on the LORD in whatever you do,
and your plans will succeed.
PROVERBS 16:1–3 NCV

The heart of man plans his way,
but the LORD establishes his steps.
PROVERBS 16:9 ESV

People can make all kinds of plans,
but only the LORD's plan will happen.
PROVERBS 19:21 NCV

We hope in the living God who is the Savior of all people,
especially of those who believe.
1 TIMOTHY 4:10 NCV

LORD, sustain me as you promised, that I may live!
Do not let my hope be crushed.
PSALM 119:116 NLT

"You did not choose me, but I chose you and appointed you
that you should go and bear fruit and that your fruit should
abide, so that whatever you ask the Father in my name,
he may give it to you. These things I command you,
so that you will love one another."
JOHN 15:16–17 ESV

Don't envy sinners, but always respect the LORD.
Then you will have hope for the future,
and your wishes will come true. Listen, my child,
and be wise. Keep your mind on what is right.
PROVERBS 23:17–19 NCV

My child, eat honey because it is good.
Honey from the honeycomb tastes sweet.
In the same way, wisdom is pleasing to you.
If you find it, you have hope for the future,
and your wishes will come true.
PROVERBS 24:13–14 NCV

I pray also that you will have greater understanding
in your heart so you will know the hope to which
he has called us and that you will know how rich
and glorious are the blessings God has promised
his holy people. And you will know that God's
power is very great for us who believe.

EPHESIANS 1:18–19 NCV

You have this faith and love because of your hope, and
what you hope for is kept safe for you in heaven. You
learned about this hope when you heard the message
about the truth, the Good News that was told to you.
Everywhere in the world that Good News is bringing
blessings and is growing. This has happened with you,
too, since you heard the Good News and understood
the truth about the grace of God.

COLOSSIANS 1:5–6 NCV

This message is the secret that was hidden from everyone
since the beginning of time, but now it is made known
to God's holy people. God decided to let his people know
this rich and glorious secret which he has for all people.
This secret is Christ himself, who is in you.
He is our only hope for glory.

COLOSSIANS 1:26–27 NCV

Trust the LORD and do good. Live in the land and feed on truth. Enjoy serving the LORD, and he will give you what you want. Depend on the LORD; trust him, and he will take care of you. Then your goodness will shine like the sun, and your fairness like the noonday sun. Wait and trust the LORD. Don't be upset when others get rich or when someone else's plans succeed. Don't get angry. Don't be upset; it only leads to trouble. Evil people will be sent away, but those who trust the LORD will inherit the land.

PSALM 37:3–9 NCV

In him we were also chosen, having been predestined according to the plan of him who works out everything in conformity with the purpose of his will, in order that we, who were the first to put our hope in Christ, might be for the praise of his glory. And you also were included in Christ when you heard the message of truth, the gospel of your salvation. When you believed, you were marked in him with a seal, the promised Holy Spirit, who is a deposit guaranteeing our inheritance until the redemption of those who are God's possession—to the praise of his glory.

EPHESIANS 1:11–14 NIV

May the LORD answer you when you are in distress; may
the name of the God of Jacob protect you. May he send
you help from the sanctuary and grant you support from
Zion. May he remember all your sacrifices and accept
your burnt offerings. May he give you the desire of your
heart and make all your plans succeed. May we shout for
joy over your victory and lift up our banners in the name
of our God. May the LORD grant all your requests.

PSALM 20:1–5 NIV

Now this I know: The LORD gives victory to his anointed. He
answers him from his heavenly sanctuary with the victorious
power of his right hand. Some trust in chariots and some in
horses, but we trust in the name of the LORD our God. They
are brought to their knees and fall, but we rise up and stand
firm. LORD, give victory to the king! Answer us when we call!

PSALM 20:6–9 NIV

But the LORD's plans will stand forever;
his ideas will last from now on.
Happy is the nation whose God is the LORD,
the people he chose for his very own.

PSALM 33:11–12 NCV

[Jesus said,] "I'll be explicit, then. I am the Gate for the sheep. All those others are up to no good—sheep stealers, every one of them. But the sheep didn't listen to them. I am the Gate. Anyone who goes through me will be cared for—will freely go in and out, and find pasture. A thief is only there to steal and kill and destroy. I came so they can have real and eternal life, more and better life than they ever dreamed of.

JOHN 10:6–10 MSG

Some of you say, "Today or tomorrow we will go to some city. We will stay there a year, do business, and make money." But you do not know what will happen tomorrow! Your life is like a mist. You can see it for a short time, but then it goes away. So you should say, "If the Lord wants, we will live and do this or that."

JAMES 4:13–15 NCV

YOUR GIFTS

God keeps showing me the same truth He has shown so many leaders throughout time. When I obey and do what I can do, God starts sending me people to fill in the gaps and do what I cannot do.

Any day now, God will make sure you meet just the person you need. The timing and resources will be so tailor-made that you will be in awe of how perfectly God worked it out. Gifted and able people, some you don't even know yet, are getting ready, waiting in the wings, to help you at just the right time in exactly the right way. Never give up because you don't know how it's going to happen or who will help you. Trust God for what you need when you need it.

**Commit your way to the Lord!
Trust him! He will act.**
PSALM 37:5 CEB

What a stack of blessing you have piled up for those who worship you, Ready and waiting for all who run to you to escape an unkind world. You hide them safely away from the opposition. As you slam the door on those oily, mocking faces, you silence the poisonous gossip. Blessed GOD! His love is the wonder of the world.

PSALM 31:19–20 MSG

The LORD is my strength and shield. I trust him with all my heart. He helps me, and my heart is filled with joy. I burst out in songs of thanksgiving.

PSALM 28:7 NLT

Satisfy us in the morning with your unfailing love, that we may sing for joy and be glad all our days.

PSALM 90:14 NIV

So let's not get tired of doing what is good. At just the right time we will reap a harvest of blessing if we don't give up.

GALATIANS 6:9 NLT

GOD gives, GOD takes. God's name be ever blessed.
JOB 1:21 MSG

From his abundance we have all received one
gracious blessing after another. For the law was
given through Moses, but God's unfailing love and
faithfulness came through Jesus Christ.
JOHN 1:16–17 NLT

But I trust in your unfailing love;
my heart rejoices in your salvation.
I will sing the LORD's praise,
for he has been good to me.
PSALM 13:5–6 NIV

"Ask and it will be given to you; seek and you will find; knock
and the door will be opened to you. For everyone who asks
receives; the one who seeks finds; and to the one who knocks,
the door will be opened. Which of you, if your son asks for
bread, will give him a stone? Or if he asks for a fish, will give
him a snake? If you, then, though you are evil, know how to
give good gifts to your children, how much more will your
Father in heaven give good gifts to those who ask him!"
MATTHEW 7:7–11 NIV

"Great gifts mean great responsibilities;
greater gifts, greater responsibilities!"
LUKE 12:48 MSG

Because he was full of grace and truth, from him we all
received one gift after another. The law was given through
Moses, but grace and truth came through Jesus Christ.
JOHN 1:16–17 NCV

Jesus said, "If you only knew the free gift of God and who it is
that is asking you for water, you would have asked him, and
he would have given you living water."
JOHN 4:10 NCV

Jesus answered, "Everyone who drinks this water will be
thirsty again, but whoever drinks the water I give will never
be thirsty. The water I give will become a spring of water
gushing up inside that person, giving eternal life."
JOHN 4:13–14 NCV

Peter said, "Change your life. Turn to God and be baptized,
each of you, in the name of Jesus Christ, so your sins are
forgiven. Receive the gift of the Holy Spirit. The promise is
targeted to you and your children, but also to all who are far
away—whomever, in fact, our Master God invites."
ACTS 2:38–39 MSG

Through him we received both the generous gift of his life and the urgent task of passing it on to others who receive it by entering into obedient trust in Jesus. You are who you are through this gift and call of Jesus Christ! And I greet you now with all the generosity of God our Father and our Master Jesus, the Messiah.

ROMANS 1:4–7 MSG

Everyone has sinned and fallen short of God's glorious standard, and all need to be made right with God by his grace, which is a free gift. They need to be made free from sin through Jesus Christ. God sent him to die in our place to take away our sins. We receive forgiveness through faith in the blood of Jesus' death. This showed that God always does what is right and fair, as in the past when he was patient and did not punish people for their sins.

ROMANS 3:23–25 NCV

I don't want to hear any of you bragging about yourself or anyone else. Everything is already yours as a gift—Paul, Apollos, Peter, the world, life, death, the present, the future— all of it is yours, and you are privileged to be in union with Christ, who is in union with God.

1 CORINTHIANS 3:21–23 MSG

Just think—you don't need a thing, you've got it all! All God's gifts are right in front of you as you wait expectantly for our Master Jesus to arrive on the scene for the Finale. And not only that, but God himself is right alongside to keep you steady and on track until things are all wrapped up by Jesus. God, who got you started in this spiritual adventure, shares with us the life of his Son and our Master Jesus. He will never give up on you. Never forget that.

1 CORINTHIANS 1:7–9 MSG

For who do you know that really knows *you*, knows your heart? And even if they did, is there anything they would discover in you that you could take credit for? Isn't everything you *have* and everything you *are* sheer gifts from God? So what's the point of all this comparing and competing? You already have all you need. You already have more access to God than you can handle. Without bringing either Apollos or me into it, you're sitting on top of the world—at least God's world—and we're right there, sitting alongside you!

1 CORINTHIANS 4:7–8 MSG

There are different kinds of gifts, but the same Spirit distributes them. There are different kinds of service, but the same Lord. There are different kinds of working, but in all of them and in everyone it is the same God at work. Now to each one the manifestation of the Spirit is given for the common good. To one there is given through the Spirit a message of wisdom, to another a message of knowledge by means of the same Spirit, to another faith by the same Spirit, to another gifts of healing by that one Spirit, to another miraculous powers, to another prophecy, to another distinguishing between spirits, to another speaking in different kinds of tongues, and to still another the interpretation of tongues. All these are the work of one and the same Spirit, and he distributes them to each one, just as he determines.

1 CORINTHIANS 12:4–11 NIV

Now finish the work, so that your eager willingness to do it may be matched by your completion of it, according to your means. For if the willingness is there, the gift is acceptable according to what one has, not according to what one does not have.

2 CORINTHIANS 8:11–12 NIV

It is the same with you. Since you want spiritual gifts very
much, seek most of all to have the gifts that
help the church grow stronger.

1 Corinthians 14:12 ncv

But the free gift is not like the trespass. For if many died
through one man's trespass, much more have the grace of
God and the free gift by the grace of that one man Jesus
Christ abounded for many. And the free gift is not like the
result of that one man's sin. For the judgment following one
trespass brought condemnation, but the free gift following
many trespasses brought justification.

Romans 5:15–16 esv

But now that you have been set free from sin and have
become slaves of God, the benefit you reap leads to holiness,
and the result is eternal life. For the wages of sin is death, but
the gift of God is eternal life in Christ Jesus our Lord.

Romans 6:22–23 niv

We have different gifts, according to the grace given to each
of us. If your gift is prophesying, then prophesy in accordance
with your faith; if it is serving, then serve; if it is teaching,
then teach; if it is to encourage, then give encouragement; if it
is giving, then give generously; if it is to lead, do it diligently;
if it is to show mercy, do it cheerfully.

Romans 12:6–8 niv

So surely we also will be punished if we ignore this great salvation. The Lord himself first told about this salvation, and those who heard him testified it was true. God also testified to the truth of the message by using wonders, great signs, many kinds of miracles, and by giving people gifts through the Holy Spirit, just as he wanted.

HEBREWS 2:3–4 NCV

Every good and perfect gift is from above, coming down from the Father of the heavenly lights, who does not change like shifting shadows.

JAMES 1:17 NIV

Offer hospitality to one another without grumbling. Each of you should use whatever gift you have received to serve others, as faithful stewards of God's grace in its various forms. If anyone speaks, they should do so as one who speaks the very words of God. If anyone serves, they should do so with the strength God provides, so that in all things God may be praised through Jesus Christ. To him be the glory and the power for ever and ever. Amen.

1 PETER 4:9–11 NIV

Christ gave you a special gift that is still in you, so you do not need any other teacher. His gift teaches you about everything, and it is true, not false. So continue to live in Christ, as his gift taught you.

1 JOHN 2:27 NCV

There is one God and Father of everything. He rules
everything and is everywhere and is in everything.
Christ gave each one of us the special gift of grace, showing
how generous he is. That is why it says in the Scriptures,
"When he went up to the heights,
he led a parade of captives,
and he gave gifts to people."
EPHESIANS 4:6–8 NCV

So Jesus came down, and he is the same One who went up
above all the heaven. Christ did that to fill everything with
his presence. And Christ gave gifts to people—he made some
to be apostles, some to be prophets, some to go and tell the
Good News, and some to have the work of caring for and
teaching God's people. Christ gave those gifts to prepare
God's holy people for the work of serving,
to make the body of Christ stronger.
EPHESIANS 4:10–12 NCV

Until I come, devote yourself to the public reading of
Scripture, to preaching and to teaching. Do not neglect your
gift, which was given you through prophecy when the body
of elders laid their hands on you. Be diligent in these matters;
give yourself wholly to them, so that
everyone may see your progress.
1 TIMOTHY 4:13–15 NIV

Go after a life of love as if your life depended on it—because it does. Give yourselves to the gifts God gives you. Most of all, try to proclaim his truth. If you praise him in the private language of tongues, God understands you but no one else does, for you are sharing intimacies just between you and him. But when you proclaim his truth in everyday speech, you're letting *others* in on the truth so that they can grow and be strong and experience his presence with you.

1 CORINTHIANS 14:1–3 MSG

And God raised us up with Christ and seated us with him in the heavenly realms in Christ Jesus, in order that in the coming ages he might show the incomparable riches of his grace, expressed in his kindness to us in Christ Jesus. For it is by grace you have been saved, through faith—and this is not from yourselves, it is the gift of God—not by works, so that no one can boast. For we are God's handiwork, created in Christ Jesus to do good works, which God prepared in advance for us to do.

EPHESIANS 2:6–10 NIV

And now these three remain: faith, hope and love. But the greatest of these is love.

1 CORINTHIANS 13:13 NIV

YOUR FAMILY

I know that God has called me to deliberately and intentionally build my life for ultimate contributions, starting with those I make in my own family. I want to leave more than a godly heritage. I want my children to leave home with a life of great faith and trust in an all-powerful God. . . . I want them to not simply know *about* God but to truly *trust* Him with all of their hearts—with their time, talent, and treasure. I want my kids to have a truly biblical worldview:- God loves all the world; we have been called to make a difference in this world He loves; it is possible to make a difference because of the greatness of God.

Let me share in the prosperity of your chosen
ones. Let me rejoice in the joy
of your people; let me praise you with
those who are your heritage.
PSALM 106:5 NLT

Think of the innocent person, and watch the honest one.
The man who has peace will have children to live after him.

PSALM 37:37–38 NCV

God, you have taught me since I was young. To this day I tell
about the miracles you do. Even though I am old and gray, do
not leave me, God. I will tell the children about your power;
I will tell those who live after me about your might. God,
your justice reaches to the skies. You have done great things;
God, there is no one like you.

PSALM 71:17–19 NCV

For he established a testimony in Jacob, and appointed a law
in Israel, which he commanded our fathers, that they should
make them known to their children: That the generation to
come might know them, even the children which should be
born; who should arise and declare them to their children:
That they might set their hope in God, and not forget the
works of God, but keep his commandments: And might not
be as their fathers, a stubborn and rebellious generation; a
generation that set not their heart aright, and whose
spirit was not stedfast with God.

PSALM 78:5–8 KJV

She is clothed with strength and dignity;
she can laugh at the days to come.
She speaks with wisdom,
and faithful instruction is on her tongue.
She watches over the affairs of her household
and does not eat the bread of idleness.
Her children arise and call her blessed;
her husband also, and he praises her:
"Many women do noble things,
but you surpass them all."

PROVERBS 31:25–29 NIV

These commandments that I give you today are to be on
your hearts. Impress them on your children. Talk about
them when you sit at home and when you walk along the
road, when you lie down and when you get up. Tie them as
symbols on your hands and bind them on your foreheads.

DEUTERONOMY 6:6–8 NIV

So God created human beings in his image. In the image
of God he created them. He created them male and female.
God blessed them and said, "Have many children and grow
in number. Fill the earth and be its master. Rule over the fish
in the sea and over the birds in the sky and over every living
thing that moves on the earth."

GENESIS 1:27–28 NCV

Then God blessed Noah and his sons and said to them, "Have many children; grow in number and fill the earth. Every animal on earth, every bird in the sky, every animal that crawls on the ground, and every fish in the sea will respect and fear you. I have given them to you."

GENESIS 9:1–2 NCV

Then God spoke to Noah and his sons: "I'm setting up my covenant with you including your children who will come after you, along with everything alive around you—birds, farm animals, wild animals—that came out of the ship with you. I'm setting up my covenant with you that never again will everything living be destroyed by floodwaters; no, never again will a flood destroy the Earth."

GENESIS 9:8–11 MSG

LORD, our Lord, how majestic is your name in all the earth! You have set your glory in the heavens. Through the praise of children and infants you have established a stronghold against your enemies, to silence the foe and the avenger.

PSALM 8:1–2 NIV

Are there those who respect the LORD?
He will point them to the best way.
They will enjoy a good life,
and their children will inherit the land.

PSALM 25:12–13 NCV

All the power-mongers are before him—worshiping!
All the poor and powerless, too—worshiping!
Along with those who never got it together—worshiping!
Our children and their children will get in on this
As the word is passed along from parent to child.
Babies not yet conceived will hear the good news—
that God does what he says.

PSALM 22:29–31 MSG

Come, my children, listen to me; I will teach you the
fear of the LORD. Whoever of you loves life and desires to
see many good days, keep your tongue from evil and your
lips from telling lies. Turn from evil and do good;
seek peace and pursue it.

PSALM 34:11–14 NIV

Thy righteousness is like the great mountains; thy judgments
are a great deep: O LORD, thou preservest man and beast.
How excellent is thy lovingkindness, O God! therefore the
children of men put their trust under the shadow of thy wings.
They shall be abundantly satisfied with the fatness of thy house;
and thou shalt make them drink of the river of thy pleasures.

PSALM 36:6–8 KJV

Good people always lend freely to others,
and their children are a blessing.

PSALM 37:26 NCV

GOD is higher than anything and anyone, outshining
everything you can see in the skies. Who can compare
with GOD, our God, so majestically enthroned,
Surveying his magnificent heavens and earth? He picks
up the poor from out of the dirt, rescues the wretched
who've been thrown out with the trash, Seats them
among the honored guests, a place of honor among the
brightest and best. He gives childless couples a family,
gives them joy as the parents of children. Hallelujah!

PSALM 113:4–9 MSG

May the LORD cause you to flourish, both you and
your children. May you be blessed by the LORD,
the Maker of heaven and earth.

PSALM 115:14–15 NIV

Ye are blessed of the LORD which made heaven and earth.
The heaven, even the heavens, are the LORD's: but the earth
hath he given to the children of men.

PSALM 115:15–16 KJV

Children are a heritage from the LORD,
offspring a reward from him. Like arrows in the hands
of a warrior are children born in one's youth.
Blessed is the man whose quiver is full of them.

PSALM 127:3–5 NIV

Oh that men would praise the LORD for his goodness, and for his wonderful works to the children of men! For he satisfieth the longing soul, and filleth the hungry soul with goodness.

PSALM 107:8–9 KJV

Praise the LORD. Blessed are those who fear the LORD, who find great delight in his commands. Their children will be mighty in the land; the generation of the upright will be blessed. Wealth and riches are in their houses, and their righteousness endures forever.

PSALM 112:1–3 NIV

You will enjoy what you work for, and you will be blessed with good things. Your wife will give you many children, like a vine that produces much fruit. Your children will bring you much good, like olive branches that produce many olives. This is how the man who respects the LORD will be blessed.

PSALM 128:2–4 NCV

The LORD is great and worthy of our praise; no one can understand how great he is. Parents will tell their children what you have done. They will retell your mighty acts, wonderful majesty, and glory. And I will think about your miracles.

PSALM 145:3–5 NCV

Kings of the earth, and all people; princes, and all judges
of the earth: Both young men, and maidens; old men, and
children: Let them praise the name of the Lord: for his name
alone is excellent; his glory is above the earth and heaven.

Psalm 148:11–13 kjv

My children, listen to your father's teaching;
pay attention so you will understand.
What I am telling you is good,
so do not forget what I teach you.
When I was a young boy in my father's house
and like an only child to my mother,
my father taught me and said,
"Hold on to my words with all your heart.
Keep my commands and you will live.
Get wisdom and understanding.
Don't forget or ignore my words.
Hold on to wisdom, and it will take care of you.
Love it, and it will keep you safe.
Wisdom is the most important thing; so get wisdom.
If it costs everything you have, get understanding.
Treasure wisdom, and it will make you great;
hold on to it, and it will bring you honor.
It will be like flowers in your hair
and like a beautiful crown on your head."

Proverbs 4:1–9 ncv

But from everlasting to everlasting
the LORD's love is with those who fear him,
and his righteousness with their children's children—
with those who keep his covenant
and remember to obey his precepts.
PSALM 103:17–18 NIV

Wise children take their parents' advice,
but whoever makes fun of wisdom
won't listen to correction.
PROVERBS 13:1 NCV

If you do not punish your children, you don't love them,
but if you love your children, you will correct them.
PROVERBS 13:24 NCV

The good people who live honest lives
will be a blessing to their children.
PROVERBS 20:7 NCV

Start children off on the way they should go,
and even when they are old they will not turn from it.
PROVERBS 22:6 NIV

Show your servants the wonderful things you do;
show your greatness to their children.
Lord our God, treat us well.
Give us success in what we do;
yes, give us success in what we do.
PSALM 90:16–17 NCV

"But you never change,
and your life will never end.
Our children will live in your presence,
and their children will remain with you."
PSALM 102:27–28 NCV

As parents feel for their children, GOD feels for those who fear him. He knows us inside and out, keeps in mind that we're made of mud. Men and women don't live very long; like wildflowers they spring up and blossom, But a storm snuffs them out just as quickly, leaving nothing to show they were here. GOD's love, though, is ever and always, eternally present to all who fear him, Making everything right for them and their children as they follow his Covenant ways and remember to do whatever he said.
PSALM 103:10–18 MSG

Do not hold against us the sins of past generations; may your mercy come quickly to meet us, for we are in desperate need. Help us, God our Savior, for the glory of your name; deliver us and forgive our sins for your name's sake.

PSALM 79:8–9 NIV

The mouths of fools are their undoing,
and their lips are a snare to their very lives.
The words of a gossip are like choice morsels;
they go down to the inmost parts.

PROVERBS 18:7–8 NIV

A wife of noble character who can find?
She is worth far more than rubies.
Her husband has full confidence in her
and lacks nothing of value.
She brings him good, not harm,
all the days of her life.

PROVERBS 31:10–12 NIV

Better to live on a corner of the roof
than share a house with a quarrelsome wife.

PROVERBS 21:9 NIV

YOUR FEARS

Whenever change is an option, fear comes calling. We must remember that the counsel fear gives will always be tainted and twisted. It is our duty to gain victory over it.

Eleanor Roosevelt, wife of the thirty-second president of the United States and a woman with a remarkable life story of her own, spoke of defeating fear this way: "You gain strength, courage, and confidence by every experience in which you really stop to look fear in the face. You must do the thing which you think you cannot do."

This is how fear has and always will be defeated. . . . That niggling feeling that you can and must choose courage and face down fear is God's Spirit in you, giving you the motivation and strength to overcome.

For God has not given us a spirit of fear and timidity, but of power, love, and self-discipline.
2 TIMOTHY 1:7 NLT

Even though I walk through the darkest valley,
I will fear no evil, for you [God] are with me;
your rod and your staff, they comfort me.
PSALM 23:4 NIV

Watch this: God's eye is on those who respect him,
the ones who are looking for his love.
He's ready to come to their rescue in bad times;
in lean times he keeps body and soul together.
PSALM 33:18–19 MSG

I sought the LORD, and he answered me;
he delivered me from all my fears.
Those who look to him are radiant;
their faces are never covered with shame.
PSALM 34:4–5 NIV

God is our refuge and strength,
an ever-present help in trouble.
Therefore we will not fear, though the earth give way
and the mountains fall into the heart of the sea,
though its waters roar and foam
and the mountains quake with their surging.
PSALM 46:1–3 NIV

Then Jesus got into the boat and started across the lake with his disciples. Suddenly, a fierce storm struck the lake, with waves breaking into the boat. But Jesus was sleeping. The disciples went and woke him up, shouting, "Lord, save us! We're going to drown!" Jesus responded, "Why are you afraid? You have so little faith!" Then he got up and rebuked the wind and waves, and suddenly there was a great calm. The disciples were amazed. "Who is this man?" they asked. "Even the winds and waves obey him!"

MATTHEW 8:23–27 NLT

But Christ, as the Son, is in charge of God's entire house. And we are God's house, if we keep our courage and remain confident in our hope in Christ.

HEBREWS 3:6 NLT

"Indeed, the very hairs of your head are all numbered. Don't be afraid; you are worth more than many sparrows."

LUKE 12:7 NIV

Pushed to the wall, I called to GOD; from the wide open spaces, he answered. GOD's now at my side and I'm not afraid; who would dare lay a hand on me? GOD's my strong champion; I flick off my enemies like flies. Far better to take refuge in GOD than trust in people; far better to take refuge in GOD than trust in celebrities. Hemmed in by barbarians, in GOD's name I rubbed their faces in the dirt; hemmed in and with no way out, in GOD's name I rubbed their faces in the dirt; like swarming bees, like wild prairie fire, they hemmed me in; in GOD's name I rubbed their faces in the dirt. I was right on the cliff-edge, ready to fall, when GOD grabbed and held me. GOD's my strength, he's also my song, and now he's my salvation. Hear the shouts, hear the triumph songs in the camp of the saved? "The hand of GOD has turned the tide!

The hand of GOD is raised in victory!

The hand of GOD has turned the tide!"

PSALM 118:5–16 MSG

Wait on the LORD: be of good courage, and he shall strengthen thine heart:wait, I say, on the LORD.

PSALM 27:14 KJV

Be of good courage, and he shall strengthen your heart,
all ye that hope in the LORD.
PSALM 31:24 KJV

Be merciful to me, my God, for my enemies are in hot
pursuit; all day long they press their attack. My adversaries
pursue me all day long; in their pride many are attacking me.
When I am afraid, I put my trust in you. In God, whose word
I praise—in God I trust and am not afraid.
What can mere mortals do to me?
PSALM 56:1–4 NIV

In God, whose word I praise,
in the LORD, whose word I praise,
in God I trust; I shall not be afraid.
What can man do to me?
PSALM 56:10–11 ESV

"Let not your hearts be troubled. Believe in God; believe also
in me. In my Father's house are many rooms. If it were not
so, would I have told you that I go to prepare a place for you?
And if I go and prepare a place for you, I will come again and
will take you to myself, that where I am you may be also. And
you know the way to where I am going."
JOHN 14:1–4 ESV

The LORD is my light and my salvation; whom shall I
fear? the LORD is the strength of my life; of whom shall I
be afraid? When the wicked, even mine enemies and my
foes, came upon me to eat up my flesh, they stumbled
and fell. Though an host should encamp against me, my
heart shall not fear: though war should rise against me,
in this will I be confident.

PSALM 27:1–3 KJV

"These things I have spoken to you while I am still with
you. But the Helper, the Holy Spirit, whom the Father
will send in my name, he will teach you all things and
bring to your remembrance all that I have said to you.
Peace I leave with you; my peace I give to you. Not as
the world gives do I give to you. Let not your hearts be
troubled, neither let them be afraid."

JOHN 14:25–27 ESV

And he awoke and rebuked the wind and said to the sea,
"Peace! Be still!" And the wind ceased, and there was
a great calm. He said to them, "Why are you so afraid?
Have you still no faith?" And they were filled with great
fear and said to one another, "Who then is this,
that even the wind and sea obey him?"

MARK 4:39–41 ESV

When the disciples heard it, they fell flat on their faces, scared to death. But Jesus came over and touched them. "Don't be afraid." When they opened their eyes and looked around all they saw was Jesus, only Jesus.

MATTHEW 17:6–8 MSG

Late that night, the disciples were in their boat in the middle of the lake, and Jesus was alone on land. He saw that they were in serious trouble, rowing hard and struggling against the wind and waves. About three o'clock in the morning Jesus came toward them, walking on the water. He intended to go past them, but when they saw him walking on the water, they cried out in terror, thinking he was a ghost. They were all terrified when they saw him. But Jesus spoke to them at once. "Don't be afraid," he said. "Take courage! I am here!"

MARK 6:47–50 NLT

An angel of the Lord appeared to them, and the glory of the Lord shone around them, and they were terrified. But the angel said to them, "Do not be afraid. I bring you good news that will cause great joy for all the people. Today in the town of David a Savior has been born to you; he is the Messiah, the Lord."

LUKE 2:9–11 NIV

We know how much God loves us, and we have put our trust in his love. God is love, and all who live in love live in God, and God lives in them. And as we live in God, our love grows more perfect. So we will not be afraid on the day of judgment, but we can face him with confidence because we live like Jesus here in this world. Such love has no fear, because perfect love expels all fear. If we are afraid, it is for fear of punishment, and this shows that we have not fully experienced his perfect love.

1 JOHN 4:16–18 NLT

Be on your guard; stand firm in the faith; be courageous; be strong. Do everything in love.

1 CORINTHIANS 16:13–14 NIV

Dear brothers and sisters, be patient as you wait for the Lord's return. Consider the farmers who patiently wait for the rains in the fall and in the spring. They eagerly look for the valuable harvest to ripen. You, too, must be patient. Take courage, for the coming of the Lord is near.

JAMES 5:7–8 NLT

Shortly before dawn Jesus went out to them, walking on the lake. When the disciples saw him walking on the lake, they were terrified. "It's a ghost," they said, and cried out in fear. But Jesus immediately said to them: "Take courage! It is I. Don't be afraid." "Lord, if it's you," Peter replied, "tell me to come to you on the water." "Come," he said. Then Peter got down out of the boat, walked on the water and came toward Jesus. But when he saw the wind, he was afraid and, beginning to sink, cried out, "Lord, save me!" Immediately Jesus reached out his hand and caught him. "You of little faith," he said, "why did you doubt?" And when they climbed into the boat, the wind died down. Then those who were in the boat worshiped him, saying, "Truly you are the Son of God."

MATTHEW 14:25–33 NIV

"The LORD your God is with you, the Mighty Warrior who saves. He will take great delight in you, in his love he will no longer rebuke you, but will rejoice over you with singing."

ZEPHANIAH 3:17 NIV

The LORD is with me; I will not be afraid.
What can mere mortals do to me?

PSALM 118:6 NIV

"But don't be afraid of those who threaten you. For the time is coming when everything that is covered will be revealed, and all that is secret will be made known to all. What I tell you now in the darkness, shout abroad when daybreak comes. What I whisper in your ear, shout from the housetops for all to hear! Don't be afraid of those who want to kill your body; they cannot touch your soul. Fear only God, who can destroy both soul and body in hell. What is the price of two sparrows—one copper coin? But not a single sparrow can fall to the ground without your Father knowing it. And the very hairs on your head are all numbered. So don't be afraid; you are more valuable to God than a whole flock of sparrows."

MATTHEW 10:26–31 NLT

"What I'm trying to do here is get you to relax, not be so preoccupied with *getting* so you can respond to God's *giving*. People who don't know God and the way he works fuss over these things, but you know both God and how he works. Steep yourself in God-reality, God-initiative, God-provisions. You'll find all your everyday human concerns will be met. Don't be afraid of missing out. You're my dearest friends! The Father wants to give you the very kingdom itself."

LUKE 12:29–32 MSG

Those who live in the shelter of the Most High
will find rest in the shadow of the Almighty.
This I declare about the LORD:
He alone is my refuge, my place of safety;
he is my God, and I trust him.
For he will rescue you from every trap
and protect you from deadly disease.
He will cover you with his feathers.
He will shelter you with his wings.
His faithful promises are your armor and protection.
Do not be afraid of the terrors of the night,
nor the arrow that flies in the day.

PSALM 91:1–5 NLT

The LORD is my rock, and my fortress, and my deliverer; my God, my strength, in whom I will trust; my buckler, and the horn of my salvation, and my high tower. I will call upon the LORD, who is worthy to be praised:so shall I be saved from mine enemies. The sorrows of death compassed me, and the floods of ungodly men made me afraid. The sorrows of hell compassed me about: the snares of death prevented me. In my distress I called upon the LORD, and cried unto my God:he heard my voice out of his temple, and my cry came before him, even into his ears.

PSALM 18:2–6 KJV

I want to immerse myself in the truth of God, and then live like I really believe it. I want to live so connected to the truth and reality of the promises of God that certain things about me are predictable. For example, since I know God will supply all my needs according to His riches in glory by Christ Jesus, no matter what the economy does, I will always tithe and be radically generous. Since I know Jesus will never leave me or forsake me, I will never give in to feelings of rejection or abandonment. Since I can do all things as Christ pours His strength through me, I will never pull back from the risks and steps of faith He places in front of me. And since I know that all of God's plans for me are for my good and not evil, I will not give in to despair no matter what happens. I am convinced that my story depends on filling myself with the truth of God and acting on it. . . .

It is easy when I have an opportunity to take a step of obedience that feels risky to talk a bigger game than I play. But when I remind myself of the truth of God—that in Christ I am an overcomer, a victor, secure, accepted, and significant—I have the courage to take the step and live out the promise.

But by shifting our focus from what *we* do to what *God* does, don't we cancel out all our careful keeping of the rules and ways God commanded? Not at all. What happens, in fact, is that by putting that entire way of life in its proper place, we confirm it.

ROMANS 3:31 MSG

Don't use your mouth to tell lies; don't ever say things
that are not true. Keep your eyes focused on what is
right, and look straight ahead to what is good. Be careful
what you do, and always do what is right.
PROVERBS 4:24–26 NCV

"Here's what I want you to do: Find a quiet, secluded
place so you won't be tempted to role-play before God.
Just be there as simply and honestly as you can manage.
The focus will shift from you to God,
and you will begin to sense his grace."
MATTHEW 6:6 MSG

And without faith it is impossible to please God, because
anyone who comes to him must believe that he exists
and that he rewards those who earnestly seek him.
HEBREWS 11:6 NIV

Don't let anyone think less of you because you are young.
Be an example to all believers in what you say, in the way
you live, in your love, your faith, and your purity. Until I
get there, focus on reading the Scriptures to the church,
encouraging the believers, and teaching them.
1 TIMOTHY 4:12–13 NLT

I ask—ask the God of our Master, Jesus Christ, the God of
glory—to make you intelligent and discerning in knowing
him personally, your eyes focused and clear, so that you
can see exactly what it is he is calling you to do, grasp the
immensity of this glorious way of life he has for his followers,
oh, the utter extravagance of his work in us who trust him—
endless energy, boundless strength!

EPHESIANS 1:17–19 MSG

I don't mean to say that I have already achieved these things
or that I have already reached perfection. But I press on to
possess that perfection for which Christ Jesus first possessed
me. No, dear brothers and sisters, I have not achieved it, but
I focus on this one thing: Forgetting the past and looking
forward to what lies ahead, I press on to reach the end of the
race and receive the heavenly prize for which God,
through Christ Jesus, is calling us.

PHILIPPIANS 3:12–14 NLT

Many sorrows come to the wicked,
but unfailing love surrounds those who trust the LORD.
So rejoice in the LORD and be glad, all you who obey him!
Shout for joy, all you whose hearts are pure!

PSALM 32:10–11 NLT

You have examined my heart; you have tested me all night. You questioned me without finding anything wrong; I have not sinned with my mouth. I have obeyed your commands, so I have not done what evil people do. I have done what you told me; I have not failed.

PSALM 17:3–5 NCV

He leads the humble in doing right, teaching them his way. The LORD leads with unfailing love and faithfulness all who keep his covenant and obey his demands.

PSALM 25:9–10 NLT

Then I confessed my sins to you and didn't hide my guilt. I said, "I will confess my sins to the LORD," and you forgave my guilt. Selah. For this reason, all who obey you should pray to you while they still can. When troubles rise like a flood, they will not reach them. You are my hiding place. You protect me from my troubles and fill me with songs of salvation.

PSALM 32:5–7 NCV

Joyful are people of integrity, who follow the instructions of the LORD. Joyful are those who obey his laws and search for him with all their hearts. They do not compromise with evil, and they walk only in his paths.

PSALM 119:1–3 NLT

Those who think they can do it on their own end up obsessed with measuring their own moral muscle but never get around to exercising it in real life. Those who trust God's action in them find that God's Spirit is in them—living and breathing God! Obsession with self in these matters is a dead end; attention to God leads us out into the open, into a spacious, free life. Focusing on the self is the opposite of focusing on God. Anyone completely absorbed in self ignores God, ends up thinking more about self than God. That person ignores who God is and what he is doing. And God isn't pleased at being ignored.

ROMANS 8:5–8 MSG

All of our praise rises to the One who is strong enough to make *you* strong, exactly as preached in Jesus Christ, precisely as revealed in the mystery kept secret for so long but now an open book through the prophetic Scriptures. All the nations of the world can now know the truth and be brought into obedient belief, carrying out the orders of God, who got all this started, down to the very last letter. All our praise is focused through Jesus on this incomparably wise God! Yes!

ROMANS 16:25–27 MSG

"Everyone who hears my words and obeys them is like a
wise man who built his house on rock. It rained hard,
the floods came, and the winds blew and hit that house.
But it did not fall, because it was built on rock."

MATTHEW 7:24–25 NCV

Jesus didn't respond directly, but said, "Who do you
think my mother and brothers are?" He then stretched
out his hand toward his disciples. "Look closely. These
are my mother and brothers. Obedience is thicker than
blood. The person who obeys my heavenly Father's will
is my brother and sister and mother."

MATTHEW 12:48–50 MSG

"Therefore, go and make disciples of all the nations,
baptizing them in the name of the Father and the Son
and the Holy Spirit. Teach these new disciples to obey all
the commands I have given you. And be sure of this:
I am with you always, even to the end of the age."

MATTHEW 28:19–20 NLT

Jesus replied, "Anyone who loves me will obey my teaching.
My Father will love them, and we will come to them and
make our home with them. Anyone who does not love me
will not obey my teaching. These words you hear are not my
own; they belong to the Father who sent me."

JOHN 14:23–24 NIV

"I loved you as the Father loved me. Now remain in my love. I have obeyed my Father's commands, and I remain in his love. In the same way, if you obey my commands, you will remain in my love. I have told you these things so that you can have the same joy I have and so that your joy will be the fullest possible joy."

JOHN 15:9–11 NCV

Peter and the apostles answered, "It's necessary to obey God rather than men. The God of our ancestors raised up Jesus, the One you killed by hanging him on a cross. God set him on high at his side, Prince and Savior, to give Israel the gift of a changed life and sins forgiven. And we are witnesses to these things. The Holy Spirit, whom God gives to those who obey him, corroborates every detail."

ACTS 5:29–32 MSG

For merely listening to the law doesn't make us right with God. It is obeying the law that makes us right in his sight.

ROMANS 2:13 NLT

When people do not accept divine guidance, they run wild. But whoever obeys the law is joyful.

PROVERBS 29:18 NLT

I obey your statutes, for I love them greatly.
I obey your precepts and your statutes,
for all my ways are known to you.
PSALM 119:167–168 NIV

My child, respect the LORD and the king.
Don't join those people who refuse to obey them.
PROVERBS 24:21 NCV

"The Father loves the Son and has given him power over
everything. Those who believe in the Son have eternal
life, but those who do not obey the Son will
never have life. God's anger stays on them."
JOHN 3:35–36 NCV

"On that day you will know that I am in my Father, and
that you are in me and I am in you. Those who know my
commands and obey them are the ones who love me,
and my Father will love those who love me.
I will love them and will show myself to them."
JOHN 14:20–21 NCV

Your decrees have been the theme of my songs wherever
I have lived. I reflect at night on who you are, O LORD;
therefore, I obey your instructions. This is how I
spend my life: obeying your commandments.
PSALM 119:54–56 NLT

Help me abandon my shameful ways;
for your regulations are good.
I long to obey your commandments!
Renew my life with your goodness.
LORD, give me your unfailing love,
the salvation that you promised me.
PSALM 119:39–41 NLT

I pondered the direction of my life, and I turned to
follow your laws. I will hurry, without delay, to obey your
commands. Evil people try to drag me into sin, but I am
firmly anchored to your instructions.
PSALM 119:59–61 NLT

I will never forget your commandments, for by them you
give me life. I am yours; rescue me! For I have worked hard at
obeying your commandments. Though the wicked hide along
the way to kill me, I will quietly keep my mind on your laws.
PSALM 119:93–95 NLT

LORD, accept my offering of praise,
and teach me your regulations.
My life constantly hangs in the balance,
but I will not stop obeying your instructions.
The wicked have set their traps for me,
but I will not turn from your commandments.
PSALM 119:108–110 NLT

Fear of the LORD is the foundation of true wisdom.
All who obey his commandments will grow
in wisdom. Praise him forever!

PSALM 111:10 NLT

Will those who do evil never learn? They eat up my people
like bread and wouldn't think of praying to the LORD.
Terror will grip them, for God is with those who obey him.
The wicked frustrate the plans of the oppressed,
but the LORD will protect his people.

PSALM 14:4–6 NLT

Do not banish me from your presence,
and don't take your Holy Spirit from me.
Restore to me the joy of your salvation,
and make me willing to obey you.

PSALM 51:11–12 NLT

As I learn your righteous regulations, I will thank you by
living as I should! I will obey your decrees. Please don't give
up on me! How can a young person stay pure?
By obeying your word.

PSALM 119:7–9 NLT

"But me—who am I, and who are these my people, that we should presume to be giving something to you? Everything comes from you; all we're doing is giving back what we've been given from your generous hand. As far as you're concerned, we're homeless, shiftless wanderers like our ancestors, our lives mere shadows, hardly anything to us. God, our God, all these materials—these piles of stuff for building a house of worship for you, honoring your Holy Name—it all came from you! It was all yours in the first place! I know, dear God, that you care nothing for the surface—you want *us*, our true selves—and so I have given from the heart, honestly and happily. And now see all these people doing the same, giving freely, willingly—what a joy! O God, God of our fathers Abraham, Isaac, and Israel, keep this generous spirit alive forever in these people always, keep their hearts set firmly in you. And give my son Solomon an uncluttered and focused heart so that he can obey what you command, live by your directions and counsel, and carry through with building The Temple for which I have provided."

1 Chronicles 29:14–19 msg

YOUR RELATIONSHIPS

You are largely the result of the people with whom you spend your time. Negative people will negatively affect you, but positive people will help you expand your story and make you more capable and knowledgeable than you could have been without them. . . .

Great people don't grow in isolation. Whenever you find one great person writing an amazing story, you will find others nearby. That's why great people have great friends. Most often, they didn't make those friends *after* they became great; they wrote parts of their story of greatness with their friends nearby. Significant people make their primary associations with people who are likeminded, focused, and supportive. They reach out to connected, influential individuals who complement their dreams and goals and nudge them on to greatness.

Because we loved you so much, we were delighted to share with you not only the gospel of God but our lives as well.
1 THESSALONIANS 2:8 NIV

Welcome with open arms fellow believers who don't see things the way you do. And don't jump all over them every time they do or say something you don't agree with—even when it seems that they are strong on opinions but weak in the faith department. Remember, they have their own history to deal with. Treat them gently.

ROMANS 14:1 MSG

"When people realize it is the living God you are presenting and not some idol that makes them feel good, they are going to turn on you, even people in your own family. There is a great irony here: proclaiming so much love, experiencing so much hate! But don't quit. Don't cave in. It is all well worth it in the end. It is not success you are after in such times but survival. Be survivors! Before you've run out of options, the Son of Man will have arrived."

MATTHEW 10:21–23 MSG

Do all things without grumbling or disputing, that you may be blameless and innocent, children of God without blemish in the midst of a crooked and twisted generation, among whom you shine as lights in the world, holding fast to the word of life.

PHILIPPIANS 2:14–16 ESV

One who loves a pure heart and who speaks with grace
will have the king for a friend.
PROVERBS 22:11 NIV

"Do to others whatever you would like them to do to you. This
is the essence of all that is taught in the law and the prophets."
MATTHEW 7:12 NLT

If anyone boasts, "I love God," and goes right on hating his
brother or sister, thinking nothing of it, he is a liar. If he won't
love the person he can see, how can he love the God he can't
see? The command we have from Christ is blunt: Loving God
includes loving people. You've got to love both.
1 JOHN 4:20–21 MSG

So in Christ Jesus you are all children of God through faith,
for all of you who were baptized into Christ have clothed
yourselves with Christ. There is neither Jew nor Gentile,
neither slave nor free, nor is there male and female,
for you are all one in Christ Jesus.
GALATIANS 3:26–28 NIV

Don't use foul or abusive language. Let everything you
say be good and helpful, so that your words will be an
encouragement to those who hear them.
EPHESIANS 4:29 NLT

And so, dear brothers and sisters, I plead with you to give
your bodies to God because of all he has done for you.
Let them be a living and holy sacrifice—the kind he will find
acceptable. This is truly the way to worship him.
Don't copy the behavior and customs of this world, but let
God transform you into a new person by changing the way
you think. Then you will learn to know God's will for you,
which is good and pleasing and perfect.

ROMANS 12:1–2 NLT

But when they measure themselves by one another and
compare themselves with one another,
they are without understanding.

2 CORINTHIANS 10:12 ESV

Don't bother your head with braggarts or wish you could
succeed like the wicked. In no time they'll shrivel like grass
clippings and wilt like cut flowers in the sun.

PSALM 37:1–2 MSG

"Love your enemies! Do good to them. Lend to them without
expecting to be repaid. Then your reward from heaven will
be very great, and you will truly be acting as children of the
Most High, for he is kind to those who are
unthankful and wicked."

LUKE 6:35 NLT

Do not let any unwholesome talk come out of your mouths,
but only what is helpful for building others up according to
their needs, that it may benefit those who listen.

EPHESIANS 4:29 NIV

Let your conversation be always full of grace, seasoned with
salt, so that you may know how to answer everyone.

COLOSSIANS 4:6 NIV

Get rid of all bitterness, rage, anger, harsh words, and slander,
as well as all types of evil behavior. Instead, be kind to each
other, tenderhearted, forgiving one another, just as God
through Christ has forgiven you.

EPHESIANS 4:31–32 NLT

Therefore, as God's chosen people, holy and dearly loved,
clothe yourselves with compassion, kindness,
humility, gentleness and patience.

COLOSSIANS 3:12 NIV

Love is patient, love is kind. It does not envy, it does not boast, it
is not proud. It does not dishonor others, it is not
self-seeking, it is not easily angered, it keeps no record of wrongs.

1 CORINTHIANS 13:4–5 NIV

Your kindness will reward you, but your cruelty will destroy you.

PROVERBS 11:17 NLT

A cheerful heart is good medicine,
but a broken spirit saps a person's strength.
PROVERBS 17:22 NLT

For God was in Christ, reconciling the world to himself, no
longer counting people's sins against them. And he gave us
this wonderful message of reconciliation. So we are Christ's
ambassadors; God is making his appeal through us.
We speak for Christ when we plead, "Come back to God!"
2 CORINTHIANS 5:19–20 NLT

Not looking to your own interests but each of you to the
interests of the others. In your relationships with one another,
have the same mindset as Christ Jesus.
PHILIPPIANS 2:4–5 NIV

"For in the same way you judge others, you will be judged,
and with the measure you use, it will be measured to you."
MATTHEW 7:2 NIV

"This is how I want you to conduct yourself in these matters.
If you enter your place of worship and, about to make an
offering, you suddenly remember a grudge a friend has
against you, abandon your offering, leave immediately, go to
this friend and make things right. Then and only then,
come back and work things out with God."
MATTHEW 5:23–24 MSG

Wives, understand and support your husbands by submitting
to them in ways that honor the Master. Husbands, go all
out in love for your wives. Don't take advantage of them.
Children, do what your parents tell you. This delights the
Master no end. Parents, don't come down too hard
on your children or you'll crush their spirits.
COLOSSIANS 3:18–21 MSG

A friend loves at all times, and is born,
as is a brother, for adversity.
PROVERBS 17:17 AMP

He who covers *and* forgives an offense seeks love, but he who
repeats *or* harps on a matter separates even close friends.
PROVERBS 17:9 AMP

"My command is this:Love each other as I have loved you.
Greater love has no one than this:to lay down one's life for
one's friends. You are my friends if you do what I command.
I no longer call you servants, because a servant does not
know his master's business. Instead, I have called you friends,
for everything that I learned from my Father
I have made known to you."
JOHN 15:12–15 NIV

Faithful are the wounds of a friend, but the kisses of an
enemy are lavish *and* deceitful.
PROVERBS 27:6 AMP

Oil and perfume rejoice the heart; so does the sweetness of a
friend's counsel that comes from the heart.
PROVERBS 27:9 AMP

Love must be sincere. Hate what is evil; cling to what is good.
Be devoted to one another in love.
Honor one another above yourselves.
ROMANS 12:9–10 NIV

Above all, love each other deeply, because love covers
over a multitude of sins. Offer hospitality to one
another without grumbling.
1 PETER 4:8–9 NIV

Make no friendship with a man given to anger,
nor go with a wrathful man,
lest you learn his ways
and entangle yourself in a snare.
PROVERBS 22:24–25 ESV

Two are better than one, because they have a good reward for
their toil. For if they fall, one will lift up his fellow.
But woe to him who is alone when he falls
and has not another to lift him up!
ECCLESIASTES 4:9–10 ESV

"If you love only those who love you, what reward is there for that? Even corrupt tax collectors do that much. If you are kind only to your friends, how are you different from anyone else? Even pagans do that."

MATTHEW 5:46–47 NLT

"And why worry about a speck in your friend's eye when you have a log in your own? How can you think of saying to your friend, 'Let me help you get rid of that speck in your eye,' when you can't see past the log in your own eye? Hypocrite! First get rid of the log in your own eye; then you will see well enough to deal with the speck in your friend's eye."

MATTHEW 7:3–5 NLT

"Don't waste what is holy on people who are unholy. Don't throw your pearls to pigs! They will trample the pearls, then turn and attack you."

MATTHEW 7:6 NLT

Don't befriend angry people
or associate with hot-tempered people,
or you will learn to be like them
and endanger your soul.

PROVERBS 22:24–25 NLT

But for those who are married, I have a command that comes not from me, but from the Lord. A wife must not leave her husband. But if she does leave him, let her remain single or else be reconciled to him. And the husband must not leave his wife. Now, I will speak to the rest of you, though I do not have a direct command from the Lord. If a Christian man has a wife who is not a believer and she is willing to continue living with him, he must not leave her. And if a Christian woman has a husband who is not a believer and he is willing to continue living with her, she must not leave him. For the Christian wife brings holiness to her marriage, and the Christian husband brings holiness to his marriage. Otherwise, your children would not be holy, but now they are holy. (But if the husband or wife who isn't a believer insists on leaving, let them go. In such cases the Christian husband or wife is no longer bound to the other, for God has called you to live in peace.)

1 CORINTHIANS 7:10–15 NLT

"If a fellow believer hurts you, go and tell him—work it out between the two of you. If he listens, you've made a friend. If he won't listen, take one or two others along so that the presence of witnesses will keep things honest, and try again. If he still won't listen, tell the church. If he won't listen to the church, you'll have to start over from scratch, confront him with the need for repentance, and offer again God's forgiving love."

MATTHEW 18:15–17 MSG

"If any of you are embarrassed over me and the way I'm leading you when you get around your fickle and unfocused friends, know that you'll be an even greater embarrassment to the Son of Man when he arrives in all the splendor of God, his Father, with an army of the holy angels."

MARK 8:38 MSG

Then he turned to the host. "The next time you put on a dinner, don't just invite your friends and family and rich neighbors, the kind of people who will return the favor. Invite some people who never get invited out, the misfits from the wrong side of the tracks. You'll be—and experience— a blessing. They won't be able to return the favor, but the favor will be returned—oh, how it will be returned!— at the resurrection of God's people."

LUKE 14:12 MSG

YOUR SALVATION

The entire Bible records God's redemptive story—God's immeasurable love, His intimate relationship with His creatures, the brokenness of sin, and the promised salvation fulfilled through Jesus. And then God's story developed and expanded through the obedient lives of trusting followers in every generation. Now is the time for you to add your chapter. . . .

There is an incredible final chapter coming for those who trust God. He has given us a preview of the triumphant finale to the earthbound part of His story, a story with no beginning or end. There is a time coming when all will be restored to the dominion and rule of Christ. . . .

Before almighty God fulfills that promise, however, He wants to empower us to live an awe-inspiring adventure.

The kingdom of the world has become the kingdom of our Lord and of his Messiah, and he will reign for ever and ever.

REVELATION 11:15 NIV

"Then if my people who are called by my name will humble themselves and pray and seek my face and turn from their wicked ways, I will hear from heaven and will forgive their sins and restore their land."

2 CHRONICLES 7:14 NLT

"If you forgive those who sin against you, your heavenly Father will forgive you. But if you refuse to forgive others, your Father will not forgive your sins."

MATTHEW 6:14–15 NLT

If we claim we have no sin, we are only fooling ourselves and not living in the truth. But if we confess our sins to him, he is faithful and just to forgive us our sins and to cleanse us from all wickedness. If we claim we have not sinned, we are calling God a liar and showing that his word has no place in our hearts.

1 JOHN 1:8–10 NLT

I'll forever wipe the slate clean of their sins. Once sins are taken care of for good, there's no longer any need to offer sacrifices for them.

HEBREWS 10:17–18 MSG

You, Lord, are forgiving and good, abounding in love to all who call to you.

PSALM 86:5 NIV

So we praise God for the glorious grace he has poured out on us who belong to his dear Son. He is so rich in kindness and grace that he purchased our freedom with the blood of his Son and forgave our sins. He has showered his kindness on us, along with all wisdom and understanding.

Ephesians 1:6–8 NLT

Then I acknowledged my sin to you and did not cover up my iniquity. I said, "I will confess my transgressions to the LORD." And you forgave the guilt of my sin.

Psalm 32:5 NIV

It is for freedom that Christ has set us free.
Stand firm, then, and do not let yourselves
be burdened again by a yoke of slavery.

Galatians 5:1 NIV

We were under great pressure, far beyond our ability to endure, so that we despaired of life itself. Indeed, we felt we had received the sentence of death. But this happened that we might not rely on ourselves but on God, who raises the dead. He has delivered us from such a deadly peril, and he will deliver us again. On him we have set our hope that he will continue to deliver us.

2 Corinthians 1:8–10 NIV

When hard pressed, I cried to the LORD;
he brought me into a spacious place.
PSALM 118:5 NIV

Since the children are made of flesh and blood, it's logical that
the Savior took on flesh and blood in order to rescue them by
his death. By embracing death, taking it into himself,
he destroyed the Devil's hold on death and freed
all who cower through life, scared to death of death.
HEBREWS 2:14–15 MSG

Then Jesus turned to the Jews who had claimed to believe in
him. "If you stick with this, living out what I tell you, you are
my disciples for sure. Then you will experience for yourselves
the truth, and the truth will free you." Surprised, they said,
"But we're descendants of Abraham. We've never been slaves
to anyone. How can you say, 'The truth will free you'?"
Jesus said, "I tell you most solemnly that anyone who
chooses a life of sin is trapped in a dead-end life and is, in
fact, a slave. A slave is a transient, who can't come and go at
will. The Son, though, has an established position,
the run of the house. So if the Son sets you free,
you are free through and through."
JOHN 8:31–36 MSG

Could it be any clearer? Our old way of life was nailed to the Cross with Christ, a decisive end to that sin-miserable life—no longer at sin's every beck and call! What we believe is this: If we get included in Christ's sin-conquering death, we also get included in his life-saving resurrection. We know that when Jesus was raised from the dead it was a signal of the end of death-as-the-end. Never again will death have the last word. When Jesus died, he took sin down with him, but alive he brings God down to us. From now on, think of it this way: Sin speaks a dead language that means nothing to you; God speaks your mother tongue, and you hang on every word. You are dead to sin and alive to God. That's what Jesus did. That means you must not give sin a vote in the way you conduct your lives. Don't give it the time of day. Don't even run little errands that are connected with that old way of life. Throw yourselves wholeheartedly and full-time—remember, you've been raised from the dead!—into God's way of doing things. Sin can't tell you how to live. After all, you're not living under that old tyranny any longer.

You're living in the freedom of God.

Romans 6:6–14 MSG

He [God] has made everything beautiful in its time. He has also set eternity in the human heart; yet no one can fathom what God has done from beginning to end.

ECCLESIASTES 3:11 NIV

And everyone who has given up houses or brothers or sisters or father or mother or children or property, for my sake, will receive a hundred times as much in return and will inherit eternal life. But many who are the greatest now will be least important then, and those who seem least important now will be the greatest then.

MATTHEW 19:29–30 NLT

"And he will answer, 'I tell you the truth, when you refused to help the least of these my brothers and sisters, you were refusing to help me.' And they will go away into eternal punishment, but the righteous will go into eternal life."

MATTHEW 25:45–46 NLT

"For God loved the world so much that he gave his one and only Son, so that everyone who believes in him will not perish but have eternal life. God sent his Son into the world not to judge the world, but to save the world through him."

JOHN 3:16–17 NLT

Jesus answered, "Everyone who drinks this water will be thirsty again, but whoever drinks the water I give them will never thirst. Indeed, the water I give them will become in them a spring of water welling up to eternal life."

JOHN 4:13–14 NIV

"I tell you the truth, those who listen to my message and believe in God who sent me have eternal life. They will never be condemned for their sins, but they have already passed from death into life. And I assure you that the time is coming, indeed it's here now, when the dead will hear my voice—the voice of the Son of God. And those who listen will live."

JOHN 5:24–25 NLT

"For my Father's will is that everyone who looks to the Son and believes in him shall have eternal life, and I [Jesus] will raise them up at the last day."

JOHN 6:40 NIV

"My sheep listen to my voice; I know them, and they follow me. I give them eternal life, and they shall never perish; no one will snatch them out of my hand."

JOHN 10:27–28 NIV

"For you have given him authority over everyone. He gives eternal life to each one you have given him. And this is the way to have eternal life—to know you, the only true God, and Jesus Christ, the one you sent to earth."

JOHN 17:2–3 NLT

But now that you've found you don't have to listen to sin tell you what to do, and have discovered the delight of listening to God telling you, what a surprise! A whole, healed, put-together life right now, with more and more of life on the way! Work hard for sin your whole life and your pension is death. But God's gift is *real life*, eternal life, delivered by Jesus, our Master.

ROMANS 6:22–23 MSG

For we know that when this earthly tent we live in is taken down (that is, when we die and leave this earthly body), we will have a house in heaven, an eternal body made for us by God himself and not by human hands.

2 CORINTHIANS 5:1 NLT

But as for me, I will look to the LORD; I will wait for the God of my salvation; my God will hear me. Rejoice not over me, O my enemy; when I fall, I shall rise; when I sit in darkness, the LORD will be a light to me.

MICAH 7:7–8 ESV

We can rejoice, too, when we run into problems and trials, for we know that they help us develop endurance. And endurance develops strength of character, and character strengthens our confident hope of salvation. And this hope will not lead to disappointment. For we know how dearly God loves us, because he has given us the Holy Spirit to fill our hearts with his love.

ROMANS 5:3–5 NLT

This is all the more urgent, for you know how late it is; time is running out. Wake up, for our salvation is nearer now than when we first believed. The night is almost gone; the day of salvation will soon be here. So remove your dark deeds like dirty clothes, and put on the shining armor of right living. Because we belong to the day, we must live decent lives for all to see. Don't participate in the darkness of wild parties and drunkenness, or in sexual promiscuity and immoral living, or in quarreling and jealousy.

ROMANS 13:11–13 NLT

The women fled from the tomb, trembling and bewildered, and they said nothing to anyone because they were too frightened. Then they briefly reported all this to Peter and his companions. Afterward Jesus himself sent them out from east to west with the sacred and unfailing message of salvation that gives eternal life. Amen.

MARK 16:8 NLT

"This Jesus is the stone that was rejected by you, the builders, which has become the cornerstone. And there is salvation in no one else, for there is no other name under heaven given among men by which we must be saved."

ACTS 4:11–12 ESV

That is why I am so eager to preach the gospel also to you who are in Rome. For I am not ashamed of the gospel, because it is the power of God that brings salvation to everyone who believes:first to the Jew, then to the Gentile. For in the gospel the righteousness of God is revealed—a righteousness that is by faith from first to last, just as it is written: "The righteous will live by faith."

ROMANS 1:15–17 NIV

Here is a trustworthy saying that deserves full acceptance:
Christ Jesus came into the world to save sinners—of whom I
am the worst. But for that very reason I was shown mercy so
that in me, the worst of sinners, Christ Jesus might display his
immense patience as an example for those who would believe
in him and receive eternal life.

1 Timothy 1:15–16 niv

"The Lord is my strength and my song,
and he has become my salvation;
this is my God, and I will praise him,
my father's God, and I will exalt him."

Exodus 15:2 esv

"Pay attention, my people. Listen to me, nations. Revelation
flows from me. My decisions light up the world. My
deliverance arrives on the run, my salvation right on time.
I'll bring justice to the peoples. Even faraway islands will
look to me and take hope in my saving power. Look up at
the skies, ponder the earth under your feet. The skies will
fade out like smoke, the earth will wear out like work pants,
and the people will die off like flies. But my salvation will last
forever, my setting-things-right will never be obsolete."

Isaiah 51:4–6 msg

YOUR SIGNIFICANCE

You might be thinking, *I'm not sure I could actually be a world-changer*. But think about this: The greatest heroes in the Bible were people we likely would not have put on our "short-list" of candidates to excel.

Remember Noah? He got drunk and humiliated himself. Abraham was old and lied under pressure, and his grandson Jacob followed in his footsteps and was a liar and a schemer. In a world that prized beauty, Leah was not beautiful, Joseph didn't get along with his brothers, Moses was timid and stuttered, Gideon was afraid and untrained, Rahab was a prostitute, Timothy and Jeremiah were too young to get respect, David committed adultery and then ordered a murder to cover it up, Elijah suffered from depression, Jonah ran from obedience, Naomi was a widow, Job went bankrupt, Peter denied Christ, the disciples fell asleep when Jesus needed them most, Martha worried about everything, the Samaritan woman had multiple divorces and lived with a man to whom she wasn't married, Zaccheus was short and sneaky, Paul was a self-righteous persecutor, Timothy had physical issues, and Lazarus was dead.

Yet, God found a way to use every single one of those people. And He did that by changing them from the inside out.

Take a good look, friends, at who you were when you got called into this life. I don't see many of "the brightest and the best" among you, not many influential, not many from high-society families. Isn't it obvious that God deliberately chose men and women that the culture overlooks and exploits and abuses, chose these "nobodies" to expose the hollow pretensions of the "somebodies"? That makes it quite clear that none of you can get by with blowing your own horn before God. Everything that we have—right thinking and right living, a clean slate and a fresh start— comes from God by way of Jesus Christ. That's why we have the saying, "If you're going to blow a horn, blow a trumpet for God."

1 CORINTHIANS 1:26–31 MSG

It wasn't so long ago that you were mired in that old stagnant life of sin. You let the world, which doesn't know the first thing about living, tell you how to live. You filled your lungs with polluted unbelief, and then exhaled disobedience. We all did it, all of us doing what we felt like doing, when we felt like doing it, all of us in the same boat. It's a wonder God didn't lose his temper and do away with the whole lot of us. Instead, immense in mercy and with an incredible love, he embraced us. He took our sin-dead lives and made us alive in Christ. He did all this on his own, with no help from us! Then he picked us up and set us down in highest heaven in company with Jesus, our Messiah.

Ephesians 2:1–6 msg

No, in all these things we are more than conquerors through him who loved us. For I am sure that neither death nor life, nor angels nor rulers, nor things present nor things to come, nor powers, nor height nor depth, nor anything else in all creation, will be able to separate us from the love of God in Christ Jesus our Lord.

Romans 8:37–39 esv

For all who are led by the Spirit of God are sons of God.
For you did not receive the spirit of slavery to fall back
into fear, but you have received the Spirit of adoption as
sons, by whom we cry, "Abba! Father!" The Spirit himself
bears witness with our spirit that we are children of God,
and if children, then heirs—heirs of God and fellow heirs
with Christ, provided we suffer with him in order that
we may also be glorified with him.

ROMANS 8:14–17 ESV

His divine power has granted to us all things that pertain
to life and godliness, through the knowledge of him who
called us to his own glory and excellence, by which he
has granted to us his precious and very great promises,
so that through them you may become partakers of the
divine nature, having escaped from the corruption that is
in the world because of sinful desire.

2 PETER 1:3–4 ESV

I have been crucified with Christ and I no longer live,
but Christ lives in me. The life I now live in the body,
I live by faith in the Son of God,
who loved me and gave himself for me.

GALATIANS 2:20 NIV

For you were buried with Christ when you were baptized. And with him you were raised to new life because you trusted the mighty power of God, who raised Christ from the dead. You were dead because of your sins and because your sinful nature was not yet cut away. Then God made you alive with Christ, for he forgave all our sins. He canceled the record of the charges against us and took it away by nailing it to the cross. In this way, he disarmed the spiritual rulers and authorities. He shamed them publicly by his victory over them on the cross.

COLOSSIANS 2:12–15 NLT

We know, dear brothers and sisters, that God loves you and has chosen you to be his own people. For when we brought you the Good News, it was not only with words but also with power, for the Holy Spirit gave you full assurance that what we said was true. And you know of our concern for you from the way we lived when we were with you. So you received the message with joy from the Holy Spirit in spite of the severe suffering it brought you. In this way, you imitated both us and the Lord.

1 THESSALONIANS 1:4–6 NLT

"You are the salt of the earth, but if salt has lost its taste, how shall its saltiness be restored? It is no longer good for anything except to be thrown out and trampled under people's feet. You are the light of the world. A city set on a hill cannot be hidden. Nor do people light a lamp and put it under a basket, but on a stand, and it gives light to all in the house. In the same way, let your light shine before others, so that they may see your good works and give glory to your Father who is in heaven.

MATTHEW 5:13–16 ESV

Put on your new nature, and be renewed as you learn to know your Creator and become like him. In this new life, it doesn't matter if you are a Jew or a Gentile, circumcised or uncircumcised, barbaric, uncivilized, slave, or free. Christ is all that matters, and he lives in all of us. Since God chose you to be the holy people he loves, you must clothe yourselves with tenderhearted mercy, kindness, humility, gentleness, and patience.

COLOSSIANS 3:10–12 NLT

Therefore, if anyone is in Christ, he is a new creation. The old has passed away; behold, the new has come. All this is from God, who through Christ reconciled us to himself and gave us the ministry of reconciliation; that is, in Christ God was reconciling the world to himself, not counting their trespasses against them, and entrusting to us the message of reconciliation. Therefore, we are ambassadors for Christ, God making his appeal through us. We implore you on behalf of Christ, be reconciled to God. For our sake he made him to be sin who knew no sin, so that in him we might become the righteousness of God.

2 Corinthians 5:17–21 ESV

Do you not know that your body is the temple (the very sanctuary) of the Holy Spirit Who lives within you, Whom you have received [as a Gift] from God? You are not your own, You were bought with a price [purchased with a preciousness and paid for, made His own]. So then, honor God *and* bring glory to Him in your body.

1 Corinthians 6:19–20 AMP

Christ is the visible image of the invisible God. He existed before anything was created and is supreme over all creation, for through him God created everything in the heavenly realms and on earth. He made the things we can see and the things we can't see—such as thrones, kingdoms, rulers, and authorities in the unseen world. Everything was created through him and for him. He existed before anything else, and he holds all creation together. Christ is also the head of the church, which is his body. He is the beginning, supreme over all who rise from the dead. So he is first in everything.

For God in all his fullness was pleased to live in Christ, and through him God reconciled everything to himself. He made peace with everything in heaven and on earth by means of Christ's blood on the cross. This includes you who were once far away from God. You were his enemies, separated from him by your evil thoughts and actions. Yet now he has reconciled you to himself through the death of Christ in his physical body. As a result, he has brought you into his own presence, and you are holy and blameless as you stand before him without a single fault.

COLOSSIANS 1:15–22 NLT

But you are not like that, for you are a chosen people. You are royal priests, a holy nation, God's very own possession. As a result, you can show others the goodness of God, for he called you out of the darkness into his wonderful light.

1 PETER 2:9 NLT

My counsel for you is simple and straightforward: Just go ahead with what you've been given. You received Christ Jesus, the Master; now *live* him. You're deeply rooted in him. You're well constructed upon him. You know your way around the faith. Now do what you've been taught. School's out; quit studying the subject and start *living* it! And let your living spill over into thanksgiving.

COLOSSIANS 2:6–7 MSG

Little children, you are of God [you belong to Him] and have [already] defeated *and* overcome them [the agents of the antichrist], because He Who lives in you is greater (mightier) than he who is in the world.

1 JOHN 4:4 AMP

If, because of one man's trespass, death reigned through that one man, much more will those who receive the abundance of grace and the free gift of righteousness reign in life through the one man Jesus Christ.

ROMANS 5:17 ESV

Through Christ you have come to trust in God. And you have placed your faith and hope in God because he raised Christ from the dead and gave him great glory. You were cleansed from your sins when you obeyed the truth, so now you must show sincere love to each other as brothers and sisters. Love each other deeply with all your heart. For you have been born again, but not to a life that will quickly end. Your new life will last forever because it comes from the eternal, living word of God. As the Scriptures say, "People are like grass; their beauty is like a flower in the field. The grass withers and the flower fades. But the word of the Lord remains forever." And that word is the Good News that was preached to you.

1 PETER 1:21–25 NLT

You show that you are a letter from Christ, the result of our ministry, written not with ink but with the Spirit of the living God, not on tablets of stone but on tablets of human hearts.

2 CORINTHIANS 3:3 NIV

How blessed is God! And what a blessing he is! He's the
Father of our Master, Jesus Christ, and takes us to the high
places of blessing in him. Long before he laid down earth's
foundations, he had us in mind, had settled on us as the focus
of his love, to be made whole and holy by his love. Long,
long ago he decided to adopt us into his family through Jesus
Christ. (What pleasure he took in planning this!) He wanted
us to enter into the celebration of his lavish gift-giving
by the hand of his beloved Son.

EPHESIANS 1:3–6 MSG

But God, being rich in mercy, because of the great love with
which he loved us, even when we were dead in our trespasses,
made us alive together with Christ—by grace you have been
saved—and raised us up with him and seated us with him
in the heavenly places in Christ Jesus, so that in the coming
ages he might show the immeasurable riches of his grace in
kindness toward us in Christ Jesus. For by grace you have
been saved through faith. And this is not your own doing;
it is the gift of God, not a result of works, so that no one may
boast. For we are his workmanship, created in Christ Jesus for
good works, which God prepared beforehand,
that we should walk in them.

EPHESIANS 2:4–10 ESV

Therefore do not be ashamed of the testimony about our Lord, nor of me his prisoner, but share in suffering for the gospel by the power of God, who saved us and called us to a holy calling, not because of our works but because of his own purpose and grace, which he gave us in Christ Jesus before the ages began, and which now has been manifested through the appearing of our Savior Christ Jesus, who abolished death and brought life and immortality to light through the gospel, for which I was appointed a preacher and apostle and teacher, which is why I suffer as I do. But I am not ashamed, for I know whom I have believed, and I am convinced that he is able to guard until that Day what has been entrusted to me. Follow the pattern of the sound words that you have heard from me, in the faith and love that are in Christ Jesus.

By the Holy Spirit who dwells within us, guard the good deposit entrusted to you.

2 TIMOTHY 1:8–14 ESV

YOUR STORY

People frequently tell me they don't believe they have a story to tell. Actually, that's impossible. The Bible teaches that your life is a letter for the world to read (see 2 Corinthians 2:3–5).

Others tell me they just *couldn't* share their story—that they don't know how or are too reserved to do so. Fact is, you *are* sharing your story. It's not that you *have* a testimony; you *are* a testimony. It's not that you *have* a story; you *are* a story. The question is, how can you make opportunities to share your story in a proactive, positive way?

Sharing your story is more than speaking—it's inviting others into your life. It is giving them the opportunity to be a part of the world-changing adventure with you. Part of the excitement of living an adventure is initiating creative opportunities to tell and show others about the life that is available to them, the life they perhaps haven't even dreamed.

But in your hearts revere Christ as Lord.
Always be prepared to give an answer
to everyone who asks you to give the
reason for the hope that you have.
But do this with gentleness and respect.
1 Peter 3:15 NIV

Then he said to his disciples, "The harvest is plentiful but the workers are few. Ask the Lord of the harvest, therefore, to send out workers into his harvest field."

MATTHEW 9:37–38 NIV

Then Jesus came to them and said, "All authority in heaven and on earth has been given to me. Therefore go and make disciples of all nations, baptizing them in the name of the Father and of the Son and of the Holy Spirit, and teaching them to obey everything I have commanded you. And surely I am with you always, to the very end of the age."

MATTHEW 28:18–20 NIV

"But you will receive power when the Holy Spirit comes upon you. And you will be my witnesses, telling people about me everywhere—in Jerusalem, throughout Judea, in Samaria, and to the ends of the earth."

ACTS 1:8 NLT

If you declare with your mouth, "Jesus is Lord," and believe in your heart that God raised him from the dead, you will be saved. For it is with your heart that you believe and are justified, and it is with your mouth that you profess your faith and are saved.

ROMANS 10:9–10 NIV

I thank my God always when I remember you in my prayers, because I hear of your love and of the faith that you have toward the Lord Jesus and all the saints, and I pray that the sharing of your faith may become effective for the full knowledge of every good thing that is in us for the sake of Christ. For I have derived much joy and comfort from your love, my brother, because the hearts of the saints have been refreshed through you.

PHILEMON 1:4–7 ESV

Therefore God exalted him to the highest place
and gave him the name that is above every name,
that at the name of Jesus every knee should bow,
in heaven and on earth and under the earth,
and every tongue acknowledge that Jesus Christ is Lord,
to the glory of God the Father.

PHILIPPIANS 2:9–11 NIV

And he said to them, "Go into all the world and proclaim the gospel to the whole creation. Whoever believes and is baptized will be saved, but whoever does not believe will be condemned."

MARK 16:15–16 ESV

For though I am free from all, I have made myself a servant to all, that I might win more of them. To the Jews I became as a Jew, in order to win Jews. To those under the law I became as one under the law (though not being myself under the law) that I might win those under the law. To those outside the law I became as one outside the law (not being outside the law of God but under the law of Christ) that I might win those outside the law. To the weak I became weak, that I might win the weak. I have become all things to all people, that by all means I might save some. I do it all for the sake of the gospel, that I may share with them in its blessings.

1 Corinthians 9:19–23 esv

For I am not ashamed of this Good News about Christ. It is the power of God at work, saving everyone who believes—the Jew first and also the Gentile. This Good News tells us how God makes us right in his sight. This is accomplished from start to finish by faith. As the Scriptures say, "It is through faith that a righteous person has life."

Romans 1:16–17 nlt

Scripture reassures us, "No one who trusts God like this—heart and soul—will ever regret it." It's exactly the same no matter what a person's religious background may be: the same God for all of us, acting the same incredibly generous way to everyone who calls out for help. "Everyone who calls, 'Help, God!' gets help." But how can people call for help if they don't know who to trust? And how can they know who to trust if they haven't heard of the One who can be trusted? And how can they hear if nobody tells them? And how is anyone going to tell them, unless someone is sent to do it? That's why Scripture exclaims, A sight to take your breath away! Grand processions of people telling all the good things of God! But not everybody is ready for this, ready to see and hear and act. Isaiah asked what we all ask at one time or another: "Does anyone care, God? Is anyone listening and believing a word of it?" The point is: Before you trust, you have to listen. But unless Christ's Word is preached, there's nothing to listen to.

ROMANS 10:11–17 MSG

You're going to find that there will be times when people will have no stomach for solid teaching, but will fill up on spiritual junk food—catchy opinions that tickle their fancy. They'll turn their backs on truth and chase mirages. But *you*—keep your eye on what you're doing; accept the hard times along with the good; keep the Message alive; do a thorough job as God's servant.

2 TIMOTHY 4:3–5 MSG

Pray diligently. Stay alert, with your eyes wide open in gratitude. Don't forget to pray for us, that God will open doors for telling the mystery of Christ, even while I'm locked up in this jail. Pray that every time I open my mouth I'll be able to make Christ plain as day to them. Use your heads as you live and work among outsiders. Don't miss a trick. Make the most of every opportunity. Be gracious in your speech. The goal is to bring out the best in others in a conversation, not put them down, not cut them out.

COLOSSIANS 4:2–6 MSG

"Stand up for me among the people you meet and the Son of Man will stand up for you before all God's angels. But if you pretend you don't know me, do you think I'll defend you before God's angels?"

LUKE 12:8–9 MSG

Therefore, brothers and sisters, since we have confidence to
enter the Most Holy Place by the blood of Jesus, by a new
and living way opened for us through the curtain, that is, his
body, and since we have a great priest over the house of God,
let us draw near to God with a sincere heart and with the full
assurance that faith brings, having our hearts sprinkled to
cleanse us from a guilty conscience and having our bodies
washed with pure water. Let us hold unswervingly to the
hope we profess, for he who promised is faithful. And let us
consider how we may spur one another on toward love and
good deeds, not giving up meeting together, as some are in
the habit of doing, but encouraging one another—
and all the more as you see the Day approaching.

Hebrews 10:19–25 niv

Then I heard the Lord asking, "Whom should I send as a
messenger to this people? Who will go for us?"
I said, "Here I am. Send me."

Isaiah 6:8 nlt

Christ did not send me to baptize people but to preach the
Good News. And he sent me to preach the Good News
without using words of human wisdom so that the cross of
Christ would not lose its power.

1 Corinthians 1:17 ncv

"Don't begin by traveling to some far-off place to convert unbelievers. And don't try to be dramatic by tackling some public enemy. Go to the lost, confused people right here in the neighborhood. Tell them that the kingdom is here. Bring health to the sick. Raise the dead. Touch the untouchables. Kick out the demons. You have been treated generously, so live generously. Don't think you have to put on a fund-raising campaign before you start. You don't need a lot of equipment. *You* are the equipment, and all you need to keep that going is three meals a day. Travel light. When you enter a town or village, don't insist on staying in a luxury inn. Get a modest place with some modest people, and be content there until you leave. When you knock on a door, be courteous in your greeting. If they welcome you, be gentle in your conversation. If they don't welcome you, quietly withdraw. Don't make a scene. Shrug your shoulders and be on your way. You can be sure that on Judgment Day they'll be mighty sorry—but it's no concern of yours now."

MATTHEW 10:5–15 MSG

God picked you out as his from the very start. Think of it: included in God's original plan of salvation by the bond of faith in the living truth. This is the life of the Spirit he invited you to through the Message we delivered, in which you get in on the glory of our Master, Jesus Christ. So, friends, take a firm stand, feet on the ground and head high. Keep a tight grip on what you were taught, whether in personal conversation or by our letter. May Jesus himself and God our Father, who reached out in love and surprised you with gifts of unending help and confidence, put a fresh heart in you, invigorate your work, enliven your speech.

2 Thessalonians 2:14–17 msg

God has given us the task of telling everyone what he is doing. We're Christ's representatives. God uses us to persuade men and women to drop their differences and enter into God's work of making things right between them. We're speaking for Christ himself now: Become friends with God; he's already a friend with you.

2 Corinthians 5:20 msg

But thanks be to God, who in Christ always leads us in triumphal procession, and through us spreads the fragrance of the knowledge of him everywhere.

2 Corinthians 2:14 esv

You're all I want in heaven!
You're all I want on earth!
When my skin sags and my bones get brittle,
God is rock-firm and faithful.
Look! Those who left you are falling apart!
Deserters, they'll never be heard from again.
But I'm in the very presence of God—
oh, how refreshing it is!
I've made Lord God my home.
God, I'm telling the world what you do!
Psalm 73:25–28 msg

But I will hope continually and will praise you yet more and more. My mouth will tell of your righteous acts, of your deeds of salvation all the day, for their number is past my knowledge. With the mighty deeds of the Lord God I will come; I will remind them of your righteousness, yours alone.
O God, from my youth you have taught me, and I still proclaim your wondrous deeds. So even to old age and gray hairs, O God, do not forsake me, until I proclaim your might to another generation, your power to all those to come.
Your righteousness, O God, reaches the high heavens.
You who have done great things, O God, who is like you?
Psalm 71:14–19 esv

I will bless the LORD at all times;
his praise shall continually be in my mouth.
My soul makes its boast in the LORD;
let the humble hear and be glad.
Oh, magnify the LORD with me,
and let us exalt his name together!

PSALM 34:1–3 ESV

I will praise you, LORD, with all my heart;
I will tell of all the marvelous things you have done.
I will be filled with joy because of you.
I will sing praises to your name, O Most High.

PSALM 9:1–2 NLT

I will tell of your name to my brothers;
in the midst of the congregation I will praise you.

PSALM 22:22 ESV

Come and hear, all you who fear God,
and I will tell what he has done for my soul.
I cried to him with my mouth,
and high praise was on my tongue.
If I had cherished iniquity in my heart,
the Lord would not have listened.
But truly God has listened;
he has attended to the voice of my prayer.

PSALM 66:16–19 ESV

YOUR TRUST

You and I were created for adventure. We were made to partner with the ultimate Author and write a heroic, fearless, and noble account. The prophet Daniel wrote, "But the people that do know their God shall be strong, and do exploits" (Daniel 11:32 KJV).

When you know God the way He wants you to know Him, you will find it much easier to choose to trust His greatness, goodness, and generosity. That trust is the beginning of radical changes in your life. Partnering with Him to write a new story will change your life, and then the new you will change your world.

Trust in the LORD with all your heart and
lean not on your own understanding;
in all your ways submit to him,
and he will make your paths straight.
PROVERBS 3:5–6 NIV

The LORD is a stronghold for the oppressed,
a stronghold in times of trouble.
And those who know your name put their trust in you,
for you, O LORD, have not forsaken those who seek you.

PSALM 9:9–10 ESV

But I have trusted in your steadfast love;
my heart shall rejoice in your salvation.
I will sing to the LORD,
because he has dealt bountifully with me.

PSALM 13:5–6 ESV

The law of the LORD is perfect,
refreshing the soul.
The statutes of the LORD are trustworthy,
making wise the simple.
The precepts of the LORD are right,
giving joy to the heart.
The commands of the LORD are radiant,
giving light to the eyes.

PSALM 19:7–8 NIV

Now I know that the LORD saves his anointed;
he will answer him from his holy heaven
with the saving might of his right hand.
Some trust in chariots and some in horses,
but we trust in the name of the LORD our God.

PSALM 20:6–7 ESV

O Lord, I give my life to you.
I trust in you, my God!
Do not let me be disgraced,
or let my enemies rejoice in my defeat.
No one who trusts in you will ever be disgraced,
but disgrace comes to those who try to deceive others.

PSALM 25:1–3 NLT

Declare me innocent, O Lord,
for I have acted with integrity;
I have trusted in the Lord without wavering.
Put me on trial, Lord, and cross-examine me.
Test my motives and my heart.
For I am always aware of your unfailing love,
and I have lived according to your truth.

PSALM 26:1–3 NLT

Blessed be the Lord! For he has heard the voice of my pleas
for mercy. The Lord is my strength and my shield; in him
my heart trusts, and I am helped; my heart exults, and with
my song I give thanks to him. The Lord is the strength of his
people; he is the saving refuge of his anointed.

PSALM 28:6–8 ESV

But I trust in you, Lord;
I say, "You are my God."
My times are in your hands;
deliver me from the hands of my enemies,
from those who pursue me.

Psalm 31:14–15 niv

Our soul waits for the Lord;
he is our help and our shield.
For our heart is glad in him,
because we trust in his holy name.
Let your steadfast love, O Lord, be upon us,
even as we hope in you.

Psalm 33:20–22 esv

Fear the Lord, you his godly people,
for those who fear him will have all they need.
Even strong young lions sometimes go hungry,
but those who trust in the Lord will lack no good thing.
Come, my children, and listen to me,
and I will teach you to fear the Lord.

Psalm 34:9–11 nlt

Trust in the Lord and do good.
Then you will live safely in the land and prosper.
Take delight in the Lord,
and he will give you your heart's desires.

Psalm 37:3–4 nlt

Commit everything you do to the LORD. Trust him,
and he will help you. He will make your innocence radiate
like the dawn, and the justice of your cause
will shine like the noonday sun.

PSALM 37:5–6 NLT

Blessed is the one who trusts in the LORD,
who does not look to the proud, to those who turn aside to
false gods. Many, LORD my God, are the wonders you have
done, the things you planned for us. None can compare with
you; were I to speak and tell of your deeds,
they would be too many to declare.

PSALM 40:4–5 NIV

"See the man who would not make God his refuge,
but trusted in the abundance of his riches and sought refuge
in his own destruction!" But I am like a green olive tree
in the house of God. I trust in the steadfast love of God
forever and ever. I will thank you forever, because you have
done it. I will wait for your name, for it is good,
in the presence of the godly.

PSALM 52:7–9 ESV

God, the one and only—I'll wait as long as he says.
Everything I hope for comes from him, so why not?
He's solid rock under my feet, breathing room for my soul,
An impregnable castle: I'm set for life. My help and glory are
in God—granite-strength and safe-harbor-God—So trust
him absolutely, people; lay your lives
on the line for him. God is a safe place to be.

Psalm 62:5–8 msg

On God rests my salvation and my glory;
my mighty rock, my refuge is God.
Trust in him at all times, O people;
pour out your heart before him;
God is a refuge for us.

Psalm 62:7–8 esv

He decreed statutes for Jacob
and established the law in Israel,
which he commanded our ancestors
to teach their children,
so the next generation would know them,
even the children yet to be born,
and they in turn would tell their children.
Then they would put their trust in God
and would not forget his deeds
but would keep his commands.

Psalm 78:5–7 niv

Your kingdom is an everlasting kingdom,
and your dominion endures through all generations.
The LORD is trustworthy in all he promises
and faithful in all he does.
The LORD upholds all who fall
and lifts up all who are bowed down.

PSALM 145:13–14 NIV

As he watched him go, Jesus told his disciples, "Do you
have any idea how difficult it is for the rich to enter God's
kingdom? Let me tell you, it's easier to gallop a camel through
a needle's eye than for the rich to enter God's kingdom."
The disciples were staggered. "Then who has any chance at
all?" Jesus looked hard at them and said, "No chance at all
if you think you can pull it off yourself. Every chance
in the world if you trust God to do it."

MATTHEW 19:23–26 MSG

"Don't let this throw you. You trust God, don't you? Trust me.
There is plenty of room for you in my Father's home. If that
weren't so, would I have told you that I'm on my way to get a
room ready for you? And if I'm on my way to get your room
ready, I'll come back and get you so you can live where I live.
And you already know the road I'm taking."

JOHN 14:1–4 MSG

Those who think they can do it on their own end up obsessed with measuring their own moral muscle but never get around to exercising it in real life. Those who trust God's action in them find that God's Spirit is in them—living and breathing God! Obsession with self in these matters is a dead end; attention to God leads us out into the open, into a spacious, free life. Focusing on the self is the opposite of focusing on God. Anyone completely absorbed in self ignores God, ends up thinking more about self than God. That person ignores who God is and what he is doing.

And God isn't pleased at being ignored.

ROMANS 8:5–8 MSG

Your life is a journey you must travel with a deep consciousness of God. It cost God plenty to get you out of that dead-end, empty-headed life you grew up in. He paid with Christ's sacred blood, you know. He died like an unblemished, sacrificial lamb. And this was no afterthought. Even though it has only lately—at the end of the ages— become public knowledge, God always knew he was going to do this for you. It's because of this sacrificed Messiah, whom God then raised from the dead and glorified, that you trust God, that you know you have a future in God.

1 PETER 1:18–21 MSG

Do good to your servant
according to your word, LORD.
Teach me knowledge and good judgment,
for I trust your commands.
Before I was afflicted I went astray,
but now I obey your word.

PSALM 119:65–67 NIV

Those who trust in the LORD are as secure as Mount Zion;
they will not be defeated but will endure forever.
Just as the mountains surround Jerusalem,
so the LORD surrounds his people, both now and forever.

PSALM 125:1–2 NLT

Hurry with your answer, GOD! I'm nearly at the end of my
rope. Don't turn away; don't ignore me! That would be certain
death. If you wake me each morning with the sound of your
loving voice, I'll go to sleep each night trusting in you. Point
out the road I must travel; I'm all ears, all eyes before you.
Save me from my enemies, GOD—you're my only hope! Teach
me how to live to please you, because you're my God. Lead
me by your blessed Spirit into cleared and level pastureland.

PSALM 143:7–10 MSG

Yes, the LORD is for me; he will help me.
I will look in triumph at those who hate me.
It is better to take refuge in the LORD
than to trust in people.
It is better to take refuge in the LORD
than to trust in princes.

PSALM 118:7–9 NLT

Let your love, GOD, shape my life with salvation, exactly
as you promised; Then I'll be able to stand up to mockery
because I trusted your Word. Don't ever deprive me of truth,
not ever—your commandments are what I depend on. Oh, I'll
guard with my life what you've revealed to me, guard it now,
guard it ever; And I'll stride freely through wide open spaces
as I look for your truth and your wisdom; Then I'll tell the
world what I find, speak out boldly in public, unembarrassed.
I cherish your commandments—oh, how I love them!—
relishing every fragment of your counsel.

PSALM 119:41–48 MSG

Do your best, prepare for the worst—
then trust GOD to bring victory.

PROVERBS 21:31 MSG

The LORD says, "I will rescue those who love me.
I will protect those who trust in my name.
When they call on me, I will answer;
I will be with them in trouble.
I will rescue and honor them.
PSALM 91:14–15 NLT

He has shown his people the power of his works,
in giving them the inheritance of the nations.
The works of his hands are faithful and just;
all his precepts are trustworthy;
they are established forever and ever,
to be performed with faithfulness and uprightness.
PSALM 111:6–8 ESV

Praise the LORD! How joyful are those who fear the LORD
and delight in obeying his commands.
Their children will be successful everywhere;
an entire generation of godly people will be blessed.
They themselves will be wealthy,
and their good deeds will last forever.
Light shines in the darkness for the godly.
They are generous, compassionate, and righteous.
Good comes to those who lend money generously
and conduct their business fairly.
Such people will not be overcome by evil.
PSALM 112:1–6 NLT

YOUR UNDERSTANDING

Not all of us are trying to find out who we are, but we should be. If you don't understand your story (your life and influences to this point in your life), you don't understand who you are and why you do what you do. You have to understand your story to leverage all your resources for positive change. . . .

Writing an "only God" story with your one and only life—a story that changes you and your world—is an impossibility unless you peel back the layers of pretense, shut down the voices and demands of others, and discern your true value and the vision, calling, and mission the Father has given you.

"Give in to God, come to terms with him and everything will turn out just fine. Let him tell you what to do; take his words to heart. Come back to God Almighty and he'll rebuild your life. . . . God Almighty will be your treasure, more wealth than you can imagine."

JOB 22:21–25 MSG

To know wisdom and instruction, to understand words
of insight, to receive instruction in wise dealing, in
righteousness, justice, and equity; to give prudence to the
simple, knowledge and discretion to the youth—Let the wise
hear and increase in learning, and the one who understands
obtain guidance… The fear of the LORD is the beginning of
knowledge; fools despise wisdom and instruction.

PROVERBS 1:2–5, 7 ESV

If you receive my words
and treasure up my commandments with you,
making your ear attentive to wisdom
and inclining your heart to understanding;
yes, if you call out for insight
and raise your voice for understanding,
if you seek it like silver
and search for it as for hidden treasures,
then you will understand the fear of the LORD
and find the knowledge of God.
For the LORD gives wisdom;
from his mouth come knowledge and understanding.

PROVERBS 2:1–6 ESV

Trust in the LORD with all your heart and lean not on your
own understanding; in all your ways submit to him,
and he will make your paths straight.

PROVERBS 3:5–6 NIV

Your word is a lamp for my feet, a light on my path.
The unfolding of your words gives light;
it gives understanding to the simple.
PSALM 119:105, 130 NIV

Do not envy the wicked,
do not desire their company;
for their hearts plot violence,
and their lips talk about making trouble.
By wisdom a house is built,
and through understanding it is established;
through knowledge its rooms are filled
with rare and beautiful treasures.
PROVERBS 24:1–4 NIV

People who have wealth but lack understanding
are like the beasts that perish.
PSALM 49:20 NIV

The fear of the LORD is the beginning of wisdom;
all those who practice it have a good understanding.
His praise endures forever!
PSALM 111:10 ESV

Your hands have made and fashioned me;
give me understanding that I may learn your
commandments. Those who fear you shall see me
and rejoice, because I have hoped in your word.
PSALM 119:73–74 ESV

How sweet are your words to my taste,
sweeter than honey to my mouth!
I gain understanding from your precepts;
therefore I hate every wrong path.
Your word is a lamp for my feet,
a light on my path. I have taken an oath and confirmed it,
that I will follow your righteous laws.
I have suffered much; preserve my life,
LORD, according to your word.
PSALM 119:103–107 NIV

Deal with your servant according to your steadfast love,
and teach me your statutes. I am your servant; give me
understanding, that I may know your testimonies!
PSALM 119:124–125 ESV

Your testimonies are wonderful; therefore my soul keeps
them. The unfolding of your words gives light;
it imparts understanding to the simple.
PSALM 119:129–130 ESV

Your testimonies are righteous forever;
give me understanding that I may live.
PSALM 119:144 ESV

Listen, my sons, to a father's instruction; pay attention and
gain understanding. I give you sound learning,
so do not forsake my teaching.
PROVERBS 4:1–2 NIV

Instruct the wise and they will be wiser still;
teach the righteous and they will add to their learning.
The fear of the LORD is the beginning of wisdom,
and knowledge of the Holy One is understanding.
For through wisdom your days will be many,
and years will be added to your life.
PROVERBS 9:9–11 NIV

Wise words come from the lips of people with understanding,
but those lacking sense will be beaten with a rod.
Wise people treasure knowledge,
but the babbling of a fool invites disaster.

PROVERBS 10:13–14 NLT

A mocker seeks wisdom and never finds it, but knowledge
comes easily to those with understanding. Stay away from
fools, for you won't find knowledge on their lips.

PROVERBS 14:6–7 NLT

People with understanding control their anger;
a hot temper shows great foolishness.

PROVERBS 14:29 NLT

How much better to get wisdom than gold! To get
understanding is to be chosen rather than silver.
The highway of the upright turns aside from evil;
whoever guards his way preserves his life. Pride goes before
destruction, and a haughty spirit before a fall. It is better to
be of a lowly spirit with the poor than to divide the spoil with
the proud. Whoever gives thought to the word will discover
good, and blessed is he who trusts in the LORD.
The wise of heart is called discerning, and sweetness of
speech increases persuasiveness.

PROVERBS 16:16–21 ESV

He replied, "You've been given insight into God's kingdom. You know how it works. Not everybody has this gift, this insight; it hasn't been given to them. Whenever someone has a ready heart for this, the insights and understandings flow freely. But if there is no readiness, any trace of receptivity soon disappears. That's why I tell stories: to create readiness, to nudge the people toward receptive insight. In their present state they can stare till doomsday and not see it, listen till they're blue in the face and not get it. I don't want Isaiah's forecast repeated all over again: Your ears are open but you don't hear a thing. Your eyes are awake but you don't see a thing. The people are blockheads! They stick their fingers in their ears so they won't have to listen; They screw their eyes shut so they won't have to look, so they won't have to deal with me face-to-face and let me heal them."

MATTHEW 13:11–15 MSG

Fools find no pleasure in understanding
but delight in airing their own opinions.
PROVERBS 18:2 NIV

The one who gets wisdom loves life;
the one who cherishes understanding will soon prosper.
PROVERBS 19:8 NIV

Though good advice lies deep within the heart,
a person with understanding will draw it out.
PROVERBS 20:5 NLT

A green Shoot will sprout from Jesse's stump, from his roots a budding Branch. The life-giving Spirit of GOD will hover over him, the Spirit that brings wisdom and understanding, The Spirit that gives direction and builds strength, the Spirit that instills knowledge and Fear-of-GOD. Fear-of-GOD will be all his joy and delight. He won't judge by appearances, won't decide on the basis of hearsay. He'll judge the needy by what is right, render decisions on earth's poor with justice. His words will bring everyone to awed attention. A mere breath from his lips will topple the wicked. Each morning he'll pull on sturdy work clothes and boots, and build righteousness and faithfulness in the land.

ISAIAH 11:1–5 MSG

This is what the LORD says:
"Let not the wise boast of their wisdom
or the strong boast of their strength
or the rich boast of their riches,
but let the one who boasts boast about this:
that they have the understanding to know me,
that I am the LORD, who exercises kindness,
justice and righteousness on earth,
for in these I delight,"
declares the LORD.

JEREMIAH 9:23–24 NIV

A truly wise person uses few words;
a person with understanding is even-tempered.
Even fools are thought wise when they keep silent;
with their mouths shut, they seem intelligent.

PROVERBS 17:27–28 NLT

He replied, "You are permitted to understand the secrets of
the Kingdom of Heaven, but others are not. To those who
listen to my teaching, more understanding will be given, and
they will have an abundance of knowledge. But for those
who are not listening, even what little understanding they
have will be taken away from them. That is why I use these
parables, For they look, but they don't really see.
They hear, but they don't really listen or understand."

MATTHEW 13:11–13 NLT

"Anyone with ears to hear should listen and understand."
Then he added, "Pay close attention to what you hear. The
closer you listen, the more understanding you will be given—
and you will receive even more. To those who listen to my
teaching, more understanding will be given. But for those
who are not listening, even what little understanding they
have will be taken away from them."

MARK 4:23–25 NLT

When I was a boy at my father's knee, the pride and joy of
my mother, He would sit me down and drill me: "Take this
to heart. Do what I tell you—live! Sell everything and buy
Wisdom! Forage for Understanding! Don't forget one word!
Don't deviate an inch! Never walk away from Wisdom—she
guards your life; love her—she keeps her eye on you. Above
all and before all, do this: Get Wisdom! Write this at the top
of your list: Get Understanding! Throw your arms around
her—believe me, you won't regret it; never let her go—she'll
make your life glorious. She'll garland your life with grace,
she'll festoon your days with beauty."

PROVERBS 4:3–9 MSG

Wisdom rests in the heart of a man of understanding,
but it makes itself known even in the midst of fools.

PROVERBS 14:33 ESV

The heart of him who has understanding seeks knowledge,
but the mouths of fools feed on folly.

PROVERBS 15:14 ESV

A wise son brings joy to his father,
but a foolish man despises his mother.
Folly brings joy to one who has no sense,
but whoever has understanding keeps a straight course.
Plans fail for lack of counsel,
but with many advisers they succeed.

PROVERBS 15:20–22 NIV

If you listen to constructive criticism,
you will be at home among the wise.
If you reject discipline, you only harm yourself;
but if you listen to correction, you grow in understanding.
Fear of the LORD teaches wisdom;
humility precedes honor.

PROVERBS 15:31–33 NLT

"Well said, teacher," the man replied. "You are right in saying
that God is one and there is no other but him. To love him
with all your heart, with all your understanding and with all
your strength, and to love your neighbor as yourself is more
important than all burnt offerings and sacrifices."
When Jesus saw that he had answered wisely, he said to him,
"You are not far from the kingdom of God." And from then
on no one dared ask him any more questions.

MARK 12:32–34 NIV

So what shall I do? I will pray with my spirit, but I will also
pray with my understanding; I will sing with my spirit,
but I will also sing with my understanding.

1 CORINTHIANS 14:15 NIV

We prove ourselves by our purity, our understanding,
our patience, our kindness, by the Holy Spirit
within us, and by our sincere love.

2 CORINTHIANS 6:6 NLT

YOUR WORLD

The message of our faith has always been that it is never, ever too late to turn things in a different direction. You cannot erase what happened in the past, but you can respond differently in the future and learn from what you have already been through. As amazing and wonderful as that is, it is also true that followers of Jesus Christ can even go further than just making the future different and better. God helps us "leverage" even the debris of our past, the hurtful things that have happened to us or the bad choices we have made, to effectively change our world.

"Still, if you set your heart on God and reach out to him, If you scrub your hands of sin and refuse to entertain evil in your home, You'll be able to face the world unashamed and keep a firm grip on life, guiltless and fearless. You'll forget your troubles; they'll be like old, faded photographs. Your world will be washed in sunshine, every shadow dispersed by dayspring. Full of hope, you'll relax, confident again; you'll look around, sit back, and take it easy."

JOB 11:13-20 MSG

But even there, if you seek GOD, your God, you'll be able to find him if you're serious, looking for him with your whole heart and soul. When troubles come and all these awful things happen to you, in future days you will come back to GOD, your God, and listen obediently to what he says. GOD, your God, is above all a compassionate God. In the end he will not abandon you, he won't bring you to ruin, he won't forget the covenant with your ancestors which he swore to them.

DEUTERONOMY 4:29–31 MSG

King David went in, took his place before GOD, and prayed: "Who am I, my Master GOD, and what is my family, that you have brought me to this place in life? But that's nothing compared to what's coming, for you've also spoken of my family far into the future, given me a glimpse into tomorrow, my Master GOD! What can I possibly say in the face of all this? You know me, Master GOD, just as I am. You've done all this not because of who I am but because of who you are—out of your very heart!—but you've let me in on it."

2 SAMUEL 7:18–21 MSG

But you, O LORD, will sit on your throne forever.
Your fame will endure to every generation.
You will arise and have mercy on Jerusalem—
and now is the time to pity her,
now is the time you promised to help.
For your people love every stone in her walls
and cherish even the dust in her streets.
Then the nations will tremble before the LORD.
The kings of the earth will tremble before his glory.
For the LORD will rebuild Jerusalem.
He will appear in his glory.
He will listen to the prayers of the destitute.
He will not reject their pleas.
Let this be recorded for future generations,
so that a people not yet born will praise the LORD.
Tell them the LORD looked down
from his heavenly sanctuary.
He looked down to earth from heaven
to hear the groans of the prisoners,
to release those condemned to die.
And so the LORD's fame will be celebrated in Zion,
his praises in Jerusalem,
when multitudes gather together
and kingdoms come to worship the LORD.

PSALM 102:12–22 NLT

But I am trusting you, O LORD, saying, "You are my God!"
My future is in your hands. Rescue me from those who hunt
me down relentlessly. Let your favor shine on your servant.
In your unfailing love, rescue me.
PSALM 31:14–16 NLT

Look at those who are honest and good, for a wonderful
future awaits those who love peace. But the rebellious
will be destroyed; they have no future.
PSALM 37:37–38 NLT

Dear child, if you become wise,
I'll be one happy parent.
My heart will dance and sing
to the tuneful truth you'll speak.
Don't for a minute envy careless rebels;
soak yourself in the Fear-of-GOD—
That's where your future lies.
Then you won't be left with an armload of nothing.
PROVERBS 23:15–21 MSG

Don't bother your head with braggarts
or wish you could succeed like the wicked.
Those people have no future at all;
they're headed down a dead-end street.
PROVERBS 24:19–20 MSG

In the last days, the mountain of the LORD's house
will be the highest of all—
the most important place on earth.
It will be raised above the other hills,
and people from all over the world
will stream there to worship.
People from many nations will come and say,
"Come, let us go up to the mountain of the LORD,
to the house of Jacob's God.
There he will teach us his ways,
and we will walk in his paths."
For the LORD's teaching will go out from Zion;
his word will go out from Jerusalem.
The LORD will mediate between peoples
and will settle disputes between strong nations far away.
They will hammer their swords into plowshares
and their spears into pruning hooks.
Nation will no longer fight against nation,
nor train for war anymore.

MICAH 4:1–3 NLT

"There is so much more I want to tell you, but you can't bear
it now. When the Spirit of truth comes, he will guide you into
all truth. He will not speak on his own but will tell you what
he has heard. He will tell you about the future. He will bring
me glory by telling you whatever he receives from me."

JOHN 16:12–14 NLT

The Spirit himself bears witness with our spirit that we are children of God, and if children, then heirs—heirs of God and fellow heirs with Christ, provided we suffer with him in order that we may also be glorified with him. For I consider that the sufferings of this present time are not worth comparing with the glory that is to be revealed to us. For the creation waits with eager longing for the revealing of the sons of God. For the creation was subjected to futility, not willingly, but because of him who subjected it, in hope that the creation itself will be set free from its bondage to corruption and obtain the freedom of the glory of the children of God. For we know that the whole creation has been groaning together in the pains of childbirth until now. And not only the creation, but we ourselves, who have the firstfruits of the Spirit, groan inwardly as we wait eagerly for adoption as sons, the redemption of our bodies. For in this hope we were saved. Now hope that is seen is not hope. For who hopes for what he sees?

ROMANS 8:16–24 ESV

For he raised us from the dead along with Christ and seated us with him in the heavenly realms because we are united with Christ Jesus. So God can point to us in all future ages as examples of the incredible wealth of his grace and kindness toward us, as shown in all he has done for us who are united with Christ Jesus. God saved you by his grace when you believed. And you can't take credit for this;
it is a gift from God.

EPHESIANS 2:6–8 NLT

Therefore I, a prisoner for serving the Lord, beg you to lead a life worthy of your calling, for you have been called by God. Always be humble and gentle. Be patient with each other, making allowance for each other's faults because of your love. Make every effort to keep yourselves united in the Spirit, binding yourselves together with peace. For there is one body and one Spirit, just as you have been called to one glorious hope for the future. There is one Lord, one faith, one baptism, and one God and Father, who is over all
and in all and living through all.

EPHESIANS 4:1–6 NLT

They are to do good, to be rich in good works, to be generous
and ready to share, thus storing up treasure for themselves as
a good foundation for the future, so that they may take
hold of that which is truly life.
1 Timothy 6:18–19 esv

What a God we have! And how fortunate we are to have him,
this Father of our Master Jesus! Because Jesus was raised
from the dead, we've been given a brand-new life and have
everything to live for, including a future in heaven—and the
future starts now! God is keeping careful watch over us and
the future. The Day is coming when you'll have it all—
life healed and whole.
1 Peter 1:3–5 msg

So roll up your sleeves, put your mind in gear, be totally ready
to receive the gift that's coming when Jesus arrives. Don't
lazily slip back into those old grooves of evil, doing just what
you feel like doing. You didn't know any better then; you do
now. As obedient children, let yourselves be pulled into a way
of life shaped by God's life, a life energetic and blazing with
holiness. God said, "I am holy; you be holy."
1 Peter 1:13–16 msg

"But before all this occurs, there will be a time of great persecution. You will be dragged into synagogues and prisons, and you will stand trial before kings and governors because you are my followers. But this will be your opportunity to tell them about me. So don't worry in advance about how to answer the charges against you, for I will give you the right words and such wisdom that none of your opponents will be able to reply or refute you! Even those closest to you—your parents, brothers, relatives, and friends—will betray you. They will even kill some of you. And everyone will hate you because you are my followers. But not a hair of your head will perish! By standing firm, you will win your souls."

LUKE 21:12–19 NLT

No, in all these things we are more than conquerors through him who loved us. For I am convinced that neither death nor life, neither angels nor demons, neither the present nor the future, nor any powers, neither height nor depth, nor anything else in all creation, will be able to separate us from the love of God that is in Christ Jesus our Lord.

ROMANS 8:37–39 NIV

The Master said:
"These people make a big show of saying the right thing,
but their hearts aren't in it.
Because they act like they're worshiping me
but don't mean it,
I'm going to step in and shock them awake,
astonish them, stand them on their ears.
The wise ones who had it all figured out
will be exposed as fools.
The smart people who thought they knew everything
will turn out to know nothing."
Doom to you! You pretend to have the inside track.
You shut GOD out and work behind the scenes,
Plotting the future as if you knew everything,
acting mysterious, never showing your hand.
You have everything backward!
You treat the potter as a lump of clay.
Does a book say to its author,
"He didn't write a word of me"?
Does a meal say to the woman who cooked it,
"She had nothing to do with this"?
ISAIAH 29:13–16 MSG

She is clothed with strength and dignity,
and she laughs without fear of the future.
When she speaks, her words are wise,
and she gives instructions with kindness.
She carefully watches everything in her household
and suffers nothing from laziness.
Her children stand and bless her.
Her husband praises her:
"There are many virtuous and capable women in the world,
but you surpass them all!"
Charm is deceptive, and beauty does not last;
but a woman who fears the LORD will be greatly praised.
Reward her for all she has done.
Let her deeds publicly declare her praise.

PROVERBS 31:25–31 NLT

Your life is a journey you must travel with a deep
consciousness of God. It cost God plenty to get you out
of that dead-end, empty-headed life you grew up in.
He paid with Christ's sacred blood, you know. He died like an
unblemished, sacrificial lamb. And this was no afterthought.
Even though it has only lately—at the end of the ages—
become public knowledge, God always knew he was going to
do this for you. It's because of this sacrificed Messiah, whom
God then raised from the dead and glorified, that you trust
God, that you know you have a future in God.

1 PETER 1:18–21 MSG